My journey from
# the Banat
## to Canada

# My journey from
# the Banat
# to Canada

NICK TULLIUS

authorHOUSE®

*AuthorHouse*™
*1663 Liberty Drive*
*Bloomington, IN 47403*
*www.authorhouse.com*
*Phone: 1-800-839-8640*

*First published by AuthorHouse   07/30/2011*

*ISBN: 978-1-4634-1836-6 (sc)*
*ISBN: 978-1-4634-1835-9 (hc)*
*ISBN: 978-1-4634-1834-2 (ebk)*

*Library of Congress Control Number: 2011910042*

*Printed in the United States of America*

*Any people depicted in stock imagery provided by Thinkstock are models, and such images are being used for illustrative purposes only.*
*Certain stock imagery © Thinkstock.*

*This book is printed on acid-free paper.*

# CONTENTS

# INTRODUCTION

Upon reaching a certain age, the reminiscences become intense and appear with increased frequency. You wonder at times, why you have never taken the time to write down these lifetime memories. There is no doubt that the people of my generation, who were born in Europe, experienced 'interesting times'. It has always amazed me, how difficult it is for so many North American descendants of Banat Swabians to imagine our lives after the Second World War, including our emigration. Many North American immigrants of the second or third generation regret that they have not asked their parents or grandparents for more details about their lives, before they left this world forever.

Such considerations led to the writing of this book. It is an attempt to describe the people, events, and landscapes of my childhood and youth in the Banat, as well as my later life in Canada. It was not my intention to present the dead or their families in a bad light, and even less to offend anybody. But it was necessary to tell the stories as they happened, and how they live on in my memory. And if there were some dark corners, incidents that were never properly explained, then I tried to find possible explanations for them. *Except for the names of my immediate family members, I have changed the names and circumstances of acting persons, so that any similarity to persons living or dead is purely coincidental.*

As a consequence of the Second World War, many Danube Swabians lost not only their immediate family members, but also their homes and homeland. They had to start over in other countries, with nothing but their skills and their willingness to work. The lives of so many of them were changed radically and often took them in completely new directions. May this book help ensure that the traces of the Swabians in the Banat, as well as their migration and integration into their new homelands, will not soon be forgotten.

Nick Tullius, Ottawa, 16.05.2011

Map of the Banat

Life is lived forward and understood backward.

Søren Kierkegaard

# 1. WHY WRITE THIS BOOK

Our ancestors have been described as people with portable roots, or as people who carry their roots with them. Around the year 1940 they still lived in the Banat, a piece of land located between the rivers Danube, Theiss and Marosch. Today they are scattered over all continents of the earth.

How this change happened, what people experienced, and how they survived is complex and no single book can do it justice. However, the experiences of one individual should reflect at least some aspects of these events and the lives of the people affected.

In focus here appear once again the people and landscapes of a time lost for ever. Resurrected from the mists of time are the villages and people of the Pannonian plains, with their lives marked by joys and sorrows, with so many individual fates, marked by so many tears.

Throughout history, the Banat was inhabited by many people. They came and they went, and more than once they were exterminated in whole or in part, by the Pechenegs, by the Tartars and by the Turks. Repeatedly the fields were overtaken by weeds and marshes spread across the western and southern parts of the territory.

After two hundred years as a province of the Ottoman Empire, the Banat was re-conquered by the troops of the German Emperor. After his victory, he called our ancestors to the Banat. They came from the southern and western regions of the empire, from Luxembourg, from Alsace, from Lorraine, from the Alpine countries and from Bohemia. They were farmers, artisans, merchants, miners and administrators.

After almost sixty years of reconstruction under a German-speaking administration, they suddenly had to contend with a shift from the large multi-ethnic state to the small one. In the century of emerging nationalism, the smaller multi-ethnic state was determined to transform itself into a nation-state. Although more people had native languages different from the new official language, they were expected to adopt the language and customs of the nascent nation-state. That the language and culture of our ancestors were those of the Imperial family and its territories did not protect them from the pressure to assimilate. In their schools they were now taught in a language that was foreign to them. Many of their native-language newspapers disappeared and their theatres closed down. Even the already abolished serfdom was reinstated, until it was finally abolished after the revolutionary events of 1848.

After the defeat in the First World War, Banaters learned that they suddenly lived in three different countries. Newly created borders separated families and possessions. Our ancestors tried in vain to understand the reasons, but they knew that they were helpless against the dictates of high politics.

During the Second World War, many Banater men lost their lives as soldiers in the armies of different countries. When the war came to an end, and even before, men and women were deported to forced labour in the Soviet Union, expelled from their country, or sent to extermination camps. The graves of these men, women and children are scattered over many parts of Europe, and all too often no one knows where they are or how to find them.

Other Banaters had found refuge in Germany, Austria, America or Australia, some right after the war, others in later years. There they created a new life for themselves, largely free from want and insecurity. The road was open for their children to fulfill their dreams; now they had a future. Our still surviving parents and grandparents, but also the people of my generation, will always carry with them the memories of their old homelands. Fortunately, the good memories are always more persistent than the bad ones. Their friends and neighbours in their new home country only seldom understand those memories and feelings.

Few members of the so-called 'experience-generation', those who lived through the war and its consequences, attempted to save their memories from being forgotten, by preserving them in writing. Those who have tried know how hard it is. It is virtually impossible for an individual to describe the variety of events and individual experiences and to do them justice. But the more of us write down our experiences, the more there is hope, that the narrative will amount to an overall picture of the people and events of our time, our stay in the Banat, and our integration into our new homeland.

# 2. PROLOG IN AMERICA

Our family story begins in 1907, when the twenty-four year old farmer's daughter Katharina Beitz from the village of Neusiedel worked as a waitress at the Tschoka Puszta inn near Kleinbetschkerek. Many farmers from the surrounding villages of the Banater lowlands used horse-drawn wagons to carry their products to the market in Temeswar. On their way there, or more often on the way back to their village, they spent a night at this inn. Many years later, the men of that generation fondly remembered their stay at the inn, and how they celebrated the successes achieved at the market.

Here Katharina Beitz from Neusiedel met farmer Johann Lukas from Alexanderhausen. He was fifteen years older, and a widower for two years. The two fell in love and married later in the same year. In the following year, a happy event took place: their son Nikolaus was born. Soon after that event, Johann was seized by a kind of entrepreneurial spirit. He sold his land and his equipment and invested the proceeds in a brick factory. The brickyard was located in Perjamosch and so the family moved to that village on the Marosch.

Meanwhile the old Beitz, Katharina's father, had moved to America. Other relatives of the Beitz family, as well as from the Lukas family, already lived in America. Uncle Thomas was not only a distant relative of Johann, but also his childhood friend. Now he lived with his wife, Aunt Barbara, in Cincinnati. From there, they wrote letters and occasionally reported with enthusiasm about life and making money in the new world. When the profits of the brickworks fell short of expectations, the decision was made to immigrate to America. The intention was to stay there for a few years, earn some money, and then decide either to stay there or to return to the Banat.

They reached Hamburg after a lengthy train ride and boarded the ship "Amerika". The ship reached New York on Christmas Eve of 1912. The festive lights of the metropolis left an unforgettable impression on Oma, as I would later call my grandmother. Uncle Thomas Beitz was already there, at the passenger terminal of the port of New York, to welcome them. He had purchased tickets for all, to continue their journey by train. When they arrived in Cincinnati, the whole extended family gathered for a festive meal, like those served at home when Kirchweih was celebrated. Soon they found an apartment in the neighbourhood and were ready to start their life in the New World.

A few profitable years followed, and the new immigrant family faithfully took its savings to the bank. Their bank account grew slowly but surely. Then another war started in old Europe. At the beginning, the people of Cincinnati hardly noticed any changes in their life and work. In 1915 a joyful event took place: After a normal pregnancy, Katharina gave birth to a beautiful little girl. Mother and father were very happy, as all parents are bound to be, when a new life begins. The fate of the child was written in the stars, and neither the parents nor anyone else could foresee it. They could not know that in just three short decades, unimaginable events would determine the fate of the child.

These emigrants were my maternal grandparents, and for the Cincinnati-born child, fate had decided that some twenty years later and in a distant country, she should become my mother.

Soon, America went to war and there was a lot of work in Cincinnati. Oma sewed shirts and blouses for a factory, and her sewing machine was humming almost continuously, day and night. Grandfather worked as a casual labourer and had a lot of free time on his hands. He met with many Hungary-German men, and at each meeting, the events in the old country were at the centre of the talks. Some of these men sold Hungarian war bonds. They asserted that these bonds would not only help their old homeland of Austria-Hungary to win the war, but would also pay interest at a decent rate. Finally, grandfather was persuaded and invested a large part of the family savings in these bonds. Oma remained sceptical and asked, "What will become of these bonds, if Hungary loses the war?" To that, grandfather could only repeat the words of his friends: "There will always be a Hungary."

As the war approached its unanticipated end, there were other concerns, in addition to those about the war bonds. Oma noticed that grandfather found less and less work. She could only watch helplessly as even his desire to work declined. Their frequent talks, initially conducted in a normal tone of voice, now ended more often with raised voices.

There were months of silence, interrupted only when the bad feelings simmering below the surface now and again broke through. One day, Oma told the assembled family bluntly: "My nerves are on end. I can not go on living like this. Unless you want to bury me here, we have to go home as soon as possible, to our Alexanderhausen in the Banat."

The surprise among the extended family members reached a crescendo, when not only Aunt Barbara and Uncle Thomas, but also their daughter Margaret expressed their desire to return to the Banat. But the biggest surprise of all was that even Heinrich Becker was ready to join the move. He was different from the rest of the family, as he had been born in Germany and came from a Protestant village in Hessen. He had met Margaret in Cincinnati, where the two of them had married. After all that he had heard in the family discussions about the Banat, that far-away place must have appeared in his imagination like paradise on earth.

# 3. Return to the Banat

Well with swing-bar

In the late summer of 1920, the three families found themselves back in the city of New York, waiting for the ship that was to take them back to Europe. They wanted to see as much as possible of the metropolis, and every family insisted to have its family portrait taken. On the portrait of our family, Oma is wearing a dress typical of the nineteen twenties, grandfather is wearing a suit with a bow tie, and my future mother is wearing a dress like any other five year old American, while Uncle Nick looks like a twelve year old boy from Cincinnati, Ohio.

In New York the three families boarded an Italian ship, which started its journey towards a final destination of Trieste. It was a long trip and many passengers suffered from sea sickness. Some of them came close to despair. Neither the trip nor the seasickness seemed to have an end. Thomas was one of the seasick and had to repeatedly lean over the railing to throw up. When the three families gathered on deck, Thomas would keep complaining in a loud voice: "If only I could drill a hole in this ship, so that it would finally sink and put an end to this misery."

Grandfather, who had been largely spared from sea sickness, replied: "Tom, the rest of us just want to get back to our village in the Banat and not go down with the ship. If you disagree, you can always jump over board. No one will hold you back."

Thomas had no answer for that and calmed down for a while. The fire-breathing mountains of Italy left a lasting impression on all, as the ship passed through the Strait of Messina. For Oma, it was the highlight of the trip home and she would still talk about it many decades later.

After the successful landing in Trieste, grandfather took care of their onward travel by rail. The trip took them through Budapest, Arad and Temeswar. The train crossed at least two new border stations that were still not completely set up. No one was counting the days or nights spent at railway stations, because all felt that the ultimate destination of the journey was near. It was Alexanderhausen, the Banat village they had missed for several years.

The arrival of the returnees was a surprise for the villagers, because nobody could have predicted the precise day of their arrival. Initially they all moved into the big house of Uncle Thomas and Aunt Barbara. During their absence, it had been inhabited by distant relatives, who now had to move back into their small house.

Grandfather soon found a house for his family. It was small and faced the meadow or cow pasture. It was actually a bit too small for the family of four, but it could be bought with the cash carried by Oma in her in her black bag. Meanwhile, the Hungarian war bonds were provisionally placed into a drawer. In time, grandfather wanted to find out how he could exchange them and get his money back. After all, they were Hungarian bonds and Alexanderhausen was now located in Romania.

# 4. A NEW BEGINNING IN THE OLD COUNTRY

Much had changed in the village. The German language had once again become the language of instruction at the village school. At the age of twelve, Uncle Nick had to transition to a German school. The skills he had acquired in Cincinnati became useless and he appeared to slowly forget his English. It was good that in America the family had always spoken their Banat-German dialect at home. He could now understand everything in the village school, but had to get used to the standard German spoken and written in school. The fate of the village teacher was actually quite similar. Although he was a child of the village, he had received his teacher training at schools in Hungary, and now had to switch his lessons to his native German.

Two years later, when my mother started school, the village school already functioned almost perfectly. The new teacher showed hardly any traces of Hungarian education and mother had not received any education in American English because she had been too young. The traces of the years that the family had spent in America slowly faded away, as its members integrated back into village life.

Oma once again wore dark skirts and blouses, like most women of the village. Mother, however, wore only so-called urban clothes that were the products of Oma's sewing machine. One day, grandfather took the war bonds from the drawer and went to Temeswar. There he handed them to a lawyer, who promised him solemnly that he would recover his money from the Hungarian government. The process dragged on for years before finally grandfather received a tiny sum of money in Romanian currency. The family would never know with any degree of certainty, how much of the new Hungarian government had actually repaid and how much had been retained by the lawyer for his services.

The years passed and after seven years of schooling mother graduated from elementary school. Now she could help Oma with the sewing and along the way become a qualified dressmaker. A second sewing machine was purchased and the two women worked well together, although Oma always remained the leader. Grandfather was now in his sixties and could only do small jobs around the house. The girls and women of the village wore more and more modern clothes. Thus our family did not get rich, but was not poor either.

Each year, work on the costumes for the Kirchweih festival began long before the date when the event would take place. Although many women and girls worked on some of these costumes themselves, a lot of work was still left for the seamstresses. Mother tried on many of these skirts and blouses and longed for the day when she would wear one herself.

A few years passed and mother was old enough to be a "Kirchweih girl". A neighbouring young man invited her to "decorate his hat" as it was called. In the photo of the couples that actively participated in that year's Kirchweih, mother can be seen standing in the middle row. She wears a beautiful implementation of the "Kirchweitracht" of Alexanderhausen. In the row behind her, stands a young man with a barely noticeable moustache. Many years later, after he had become my father, this young man still claimed that, of all participating "Kirchweih girls" of that year, mother was the fairest one of all.

The two were married the following year, after father had completed his carpentry apprenticeship as a master. His mother, my other grandmother, had already been widow for eight years, and was pleased to see the success of her oldest son. He and his cousin, my Schneider Uncle, were always the best in their class, but the parents of both lacked the money necessary for sending them to higher schools. My father did not want to become a farm hand, and to learn a trade was the only option available to him.

The family legend has it that very early on my parents made a decision: They would have only one child, as did so many of their friends and classmates. For the first time in the history of the family, the child would get a chance to attend as many schools as his abilities would justify.

# 5. Birth and survival

- Oma - Katharina Lukas, née Beitz

My grandparents exchanged their little house facing the meadow, for a slightly larger and more centrally located house. It was situated in the western quadrant of the village, only six houses away from the main street. It had three windows facing the street, one each for the front room, the kitchen, and the back room. Grandma was very happy with the front room, because it had two windows on the gable end and one on each side. In this bright room, sewing was a real joy. The court-side veranda was covered with red and white square tiles and had a chest-high wall. On one of its ends was the storage room, with its door next to the main entrance, which was the kitchen door. On the other side of the kitchen door, was the heavy door that led to the attic. That door had, of course, a large lock with the largest of our many keys.

Between the house and the secondary building, there was the courtyard, paved with burned brick. In the middle of the courtyard stood the well surrounded with a wooden enclosure, with its high swing-bar towering above it all. The secondary building housed the summer kitchen, my father's workshop, a large barn open on two sides, with a mighty pillar at the corner formed by the open sides. The two stables were attached to the secondary building and ran toward the backyard and garden. Their red tiled roof extended downward at a constant slope, away from the secondary building that was covered with grey roof tiles of an older vintage.

In this house I was born, with the help of a midwife, on a fine October day, in the year following my parents' marriage. It was many years later that I learned about the very bad cold that I contracted in the second winter of my life, and that had come very close to ending my life. It weakened me so much, that I was unable to eat or drink. After a thorough examination, Dr. Wetzler, our village physician, announced to my parents and grandparents that he could do nothing more for me. Mother cried, but Oma did not give up hope. She took care of me and kept me alive through the rest of the day and the night, with lemon juice and a few drops of milk. It is said, that after a peaceful sleep, I was again able to smile to the world.

Sometimes memories from early childhood appear like flashes, but they are rare and they are short. My other grandmother, my father's mother lived with my Uncle Johann and his family at the other end of the village. It was on a Christmas Eve that my father and I walked there, allegedly to pick up some milk. There were two small children in their house, both younger than I. The little boy was my cousin Hans and the baby was my cousin Katarina, whom everybody called Kathi.

On our way home, my father drew my attention to the evening sky. Where the sun had just set, some large red stripes stood in the sky. My father explained that the Christ Child was baking cakes. On this enchanted evening, I was ready to believe it. When we re-entered our house, a Christmas tree was standing in the front room, festively decorated with lit candles and homemade candies. Mother and Oma told us that we had just missed the Christ Child. It had just left the house but had left behind the Christmas tree and the gifts underneath. Under the Christmas tree, the gifts were neatly arranged: apples, oranges, candies and toys. And, since a war was going on somewhere, there was a miniature toy car, to which cannon was attached. The car had a spring-operated engine. After winding up the spring, the car was racing across the wooden floor of the front room, with its cannon firing away. I took good care of the toy, so it was racing down the room and veranda for a few more years. By the time it no longer worked, we already had real military trucks and guns in the village.

The summers were long, hot and full of dust. In the middle of the street, the deep tracks made by horse-drawn wagons were filled with a couple of inches of fine dust. My friend Richard and I ran side by side along these tracks, dragging our feet, and kicking up an impressive cloud of dust behind us. In the evening, after the sun had set, we had to conclude the day by taking a full bath in the trough located next to the well with the swing-bar that had been warmed up by the sun all day.

There was at least one neighbour who found our runs in front of the dust cloud very funny. Kaspar was a few years older than us and he was different than the other boys of the village. After doing very well in the village school, he had been sent on to higher education. From there he had returned without any degree or title. Most villagers regarded him as highly intelligent, but many added that he was also a little crazy. He always seemed to have time for me and I always liked to listen to him, because he could answer any questions and provide an explanation for everything.

I always regarded our Uncle Gerhard as an exceptional man. He was actually the half-uncle of my mother and some people in the village said about him that he was something like a communist or socialist. I had only a vague idea of what that was, but it sounded weird in my ears. There were actually several men the village to whom this epithet was attributed. During or after the First World War, they had been prisoners of war in Russia, where they had experienced the October Revolution. Uncle Gerhard liked to tell stories about bear hunts in the Urals, and about his liberation and fraternization with the local population. After his return, he was one of the first owners of a radio in the village, and listened regularly to the German-language programs of Radio Moscow. Talking to my father, he drew a bright picture of the future socialist village: "We will all work together, in our large and undivided fields, after we overcome the absurd division into tiny individual parcels. We will all be equal and work together as brothers. We will sing and be merry, because no one will urge us on. And we will be rewarded according to our accomplishments. There will be neither poor nor rich, but all will live worry free."

My father could not hide his amazement, because Uncle Gerhard was certainly not a proletarian. He was actually one of the rich in the village, because he owned not only many acres of land, but also a corn mill, a tractor and a threshing machine.

The corn mill was driven by a diesel engine that was state of the art for its time. It had a powerful, horizontally mounted cylinder and a huge flywheel. Uncle Gerhard was universally admired, as he regularly overhauled this engine by dismantling it into its smallest components and then putting it back together again. The villager admired his capability and wondered where he had acquired such knowledge, for he had attended only the village school.

It was not easy to start the engine in winter; the oil had to be warmed up beforehand. This could only be done by draining it into a bucket and placing it on the kitchen stove. After Uncle Gerhard was drafted into the army, his wife Christina did her best to keep the corn mill in operation. On a cold day in January, a misfortune happened. When she pulled the oil-filled bucket from the stove, it overturned and caught fire. Christina received severe burns and eventually died of the consequences. How long Uncle Gerhard carried this suffering with him, nobody knew.

I remember the large L-shaped corner building in which Uncle Gerhard and his extended family lived. The household duties had been taken on by his daughter Gertrude, married to Adam Gilde. Their son Hermann was two years older, while her daughter Hilde was two years younger than I.

Our village priest, Johann Molnar, enjoyed great respect in the village, as a very learned man who was always ready with advice and assistance. Everyone knew that he came from Perjamosch and had completed his degree as a lawyer. After his fiancée was drowned while bathing in the Marosch, he decided to become a priest. At the dedication of the heroes' monument he had delivered a sermon that remained unforgettable for everyone present. In it he described the atrocities and the unimaginable horrors of the Great War and its consequences for the bereaved and for the entire civilized world. He concluded with the words: "Never, never again war!" Many of the women wept aloud, and even the men had tears in their eyes. The Chairman of the church council, farmer Wambach, whispered to the priest: "Say it again, sir". Dr. Molnar just shook his head and said: "That I cannot do."

Since then, everyone knew that priest Molnar was a man of peace. Kaspar said with admiration that the priest was a pacifist. Later priest Molnar also acquired a radio and listened to the broadcasts of the British Broadcasting Company. In some of his later sermons, he is said to have even quoted Winston Churchill. When the new organizations called "German Men's Team" and "German Ethnic Group" established themselves in the village, he was attacked by both. Many of the villagers found it very difficult to decide if they were for or against one or another of these parties.

# 6.  STARTING SCHOOL

One day we were sitting in kindergarten, on small stools, and the kindergarten teacher told us fairy tales. We had to call her Miss and she talked to us in standard German rather than in the dialect we used at home. At Easter, we searched the backyard of the kindergarten for hidden Easter eggs, and once a year we amused our parents with a show presented in a large hall. One summer, so-called "harvest kindergarten" was introduced. We had to spend a few summer weeks in kindergarten, while our parents were busy with the harvest. After lunch, our curriculum prescribed a nap, a kind of siesta in the darkened room. I was not used to sleeping after lunch, so I did not accept the imposition. I received permission to spend noon hour in the large sand pile placed in the kindergarten backyard. There I sat alone, all the sand was mine and I could build whatever I wanted.

In one of those years, quite unexpectedly, we had flooding in our village. A pond called Clemens-Kaul, located very close to some houses of the village, filled up with water, which threatened to flood those houses. Pumps were brought in to move the water from the Clemens-Kaul to another pond called Sandkaul, which was located further away from the village. In the Sandkaul, some villagers used their wooden troughs for boat rides. One afternoon, when no adults were around, two boys from the neighbourhood wanted to try out the boat rides. After they rowed themselves to the centre of the water, their improvised boat capsized and they fell into the water. Like most boys from the village, they did not know how to swim. They screamed for help and one of the two was rescued by a neighbour. The second boy, a student in our class, could not be saved and drowned. Our entire class took part in the funeral. I still remember the sad sounds of brass band, as they played their march for the dead; it brought me close to tears. I found the event ultimately incomprehensible: How could God put a sudden end to the life of such a young boy? Where was the boy's guardian angel?

Our kindergarten was located right next to the big inn, with the school located opposite the inn, on the other side of Main Street. One day the main street was full of cars, mostly trucks. They were brand new and all had the same dark green color. The excitement in the village was great, for the soldiers, who were sitting on the cars, spoke German. We children would not miss this unprecedented event. Some of us were standing in front of the school and had to cross the main road to get back to the kindergarten. On our side, a number of trucks stood in a long row, obscuring Main Street. Now and then, other cars went past them. I wanted to run across the street, but had the misfortune of colliding with an oncoming truck. All went dark in front of my eyes. When I regained consciousness, I sat on a kindergarten-chair, with my head bent backwards, and with a bleeding nose. I never had another nosebleed, neither before nor after this mishap.

I did not mention this incident at home, as I wanted to avoid a sermon on caution and watching out for myself, from both parents and grandparents. But Oma had some shopping to do and met Kaspar. He asked her innocently, how I was doing after the accident. As Grandma knew nothing about it, he told her the story of how I was hit by a truck, and how the driver of the truck stepped on his brakes with such force, that the rear of his car rose a foot into the air. Grandma came home excited and examined me thoroughly. I could not entirely get away without a scolding. When I later reproached Kaspar for betraying me, he said that sooner or later Oma and my parents would have found out about the accident anyway. And he comforted me with the thought that a merciful fate has just kept me alive for greater things to come. I did not believe a word of what he said; it was just a coincidence, an event without any special meaning, as it can be expected to occur in the lives of most people.

The soldiers were billeted for a time in our village. They were mostly good-looking young boys and they sang beautiful German songs. For most villagers, it was an once-in-a-lifetime experience to meet soldiers who spoke our language and sang our songs. As a group marched through the village and sang the song about Erika, our neighbour Maria stood at the edge of the street, wiping her tears on her apron. She repeated time after time: "Our soldiers! These are our soldiers!"

One of the shiny new trucks was parked in our yard and its soldiers spoiled me with their military rye bread. One fine morning, the whole column began moving out of the village. It was said that they went to

Serbia, because war had broken out in that country. Maria was standing next to mother and Oma on the street and she was crying: "The poor boys! They are too young to lose their lives in this war have. But why? For what reason?"

I did not quite understand what she meant and how she knew their fate. After all, they were healthy young men, full of vigour and optimism and the will to live. No one could know then, not even Maria herself, how quickly her prophecy would come true.

In the autumn, my mother and I stood in the office of principal Bachus to enrol me in the first grade. But as I would reach the required age only in October, a medical certificate was necessary to confirm that I was mature enough to start school. We walked the short distance to the office of Dr. Wetzler and received the required certificate. With that paper in hand, I was enrolled and the classes could start.

In first grade we used slate pencils to write the Gothic letters on our small slate tablets. Attached by a string to each slate tablet was a sponge, used to wipe out any text, whether it was right or wrong. Our teacher was old, and my father told me that he had been trained in the Austria-Hungarian times and knew how to teach Hungarian better than German. We first-graders often found his pronunciation funny and giggled a lot.

In second grade, things had changed radically. Our class teacher was none other than principal Bachus himself. The school desks were now equipped with ink wells and we wrote with steel pens into lined notebooks. Each student received a pre-printed page with the heading "Normal Written German". The page contained the small and the large letters of the alphabet and the numbers from zero to nine. Every day we had to write a full page of twelve lines, and any mistake or inkblot earned the offender a blow with the rod on the butt.

This went on for a while, before the procedure one day suddenly stopped. What had happened? One of the girls had been subjected to the procedure so often that she could barely sit on the school bench. Her father was a strong farmer and the rumour was that one evening in the darkness he had grabbed principal Bachus by the collar and made him an offer that he could not refuse. The next day, corporal punishment for writing mistakes and ink mishaps was abolished and never mentioned again.

But principal Bachus was still not finished with his new teaching methods. One day he wrote on the big blackboard the sentence: "Five minutes before appointment time—that is the German punctuality". To make sure that we would not forget this phrase, we first had to write it down repeatedly, to fill an entire notebook page. Then Bachus explained to us, that we had to be in the classroom five minutes before eight o'clock, not earlier and not later. Being late had always been frowned upon, but being too early was a brand new requirement.

The next day the boys from the seventh grade were given the task of walking through the streets fifteen minutes to eight, to capture all early risers. I was among the youngsters from our section of the village that saw the newly appointed overseers walking back and forth on the main street, and hid behind the thick mulberry trees. We did not want to be captured and taken to principal Bachus. We waited until the seventh-graders had disappeared from the main street, before going to school. All of us were late. Like most students, I had never been late to school before that day. Now we stood in a long line in the school corridor to stretch out our right hands so that principal Bachus could hit it with the rod. This method was also discontinued and the mandate of the guards abolished, but the definition of punctuality remained written on the blackboard in our classroom for a long time thereafter.

Another innovation also had unforeseen consequences. According to a long established custom, the children greeted all adults in the village with „Grüß Gott". One day, principal Bachus instructed us students that we now had to use the "German greeting", shorthand for "Heil Hitler". This struck most of us as highly unusual, because we had just grown up with the „Grüß Gott", as had our parents and grandparents before us. When a classmate surprised my old Uncle Gerhard with the new greeting, Gerhard took the boy's cap from his head and told him: "Now you step back, and return with the proper greeting!"

The boy went back a few steps, then turned around, said his „Grüß Gott" and received his cap again. He arrived at school all excited and recounted his experience to all classmates. We were now confused and did not know how to greet people properly. When we saw Uncle Gerhard on the street, we did not want to take any chances: We crossed over to the other side of the street instead.

One day, on our way home from school, we encountered an unusual band of riders. The men on horses wore high-gloss boots, white shirts under black jackets, but no hats. They trotted around the main street and around the Rondell, as if to shock other people. Many people were indeed shocked, but none more than priest Molnar. It was after all a novelty: The rich farmer Spanagel celebrated a church-independent wedding for his son, as introduced by "the Party", whatever that was. It was unheard of: a wedding without church. In his next Sunday sermon priest Molnar talked about the new heathens, and reminded them of the terrible consequences of war, which always hit the little people hardest.

The conversation of the adults then turned to the fact that the Ethnic Group had taken over our schools. In reply to my question, Kaspar told me that the so-called Ethnic Group had assumed leadership of the institutions of all Germans in Romania. In the village, the Ethnic Group had taken over only one room in the building of the Great Inn. In time it became apparent that more was behind it, much more. A neighbouring farmer was sent somewhere for training and when he returned, he was appointed local leader of the Ethnic Group. Kaspar explained that the local leader was required by his superiors to hold meetings for the young men in order to familiarize them with the Ethnic Group and its goals. Kaspar had participated in only one of these meetings, after which he just refused to attend any more. Because he was different, he could afford to do what most young men could not do.

The changes came to light only slowly, but eventually the word got around. It was said that the men who had been spared by the war until now, would soon have to join the military. Most of the men had already spent time in the Romanian army before. For some it had been a good experience and they were satisfied with their treatment. For others the experience had been bad and they did not want to repeat it. Now they were supposed to be able to decide for themselves whether they wanted to join the German or the Romanian military. Local leader Wirth was adamant in his meetings, that the Germans of Romania, as members of the great German nation, had the sacred duty to fight for Germany, and they could do that best by joining the armed forces of the German Reich. In one of these meetings, farmer Roth stood up and said that, as the Romanian army fought alongside the German armed forces, he wanted to obey his already received order and join his Romanian unit. Others thought the same, but followed the famous saying: Speech is silver, silence is golden.

The next morning, on our way to school, my friend Richard and I passed the house of the farmer Roth. We noticed with bewilderment that some windows were broken and that someone had thrown a number of eggs against the house. We children were astonished, because we had never seen anything like this in our village. When we told our parents about it, they just shook their heads and did not say a word.

# 7.  THE INVOLUNTARY VOLUNTEERS

The news spread like wildfire in the village that several men had been ordered to report to their units of the Romanian army. It was learned that Bauer Roth and some others had already joined their units in Old Romania. They had acted according to the old adage, that you should always prefer the known evil to the unknown one. Not unexpectedly, my father received his call-up within a few days. With mother's help, he packed his bags and boarded the early train to Temeswar in order to continue on to his unit.

Then the days passed, and after them the weeks, without hearing even a peep from him. He had disappeared from the face of the earth, but mother and Oma assumed that he was in Germany. Night after night I accompanied my mother to the post office next to the elementary school. Every evening we returned home without a letter or even a postcard from him. After three weeks, we finally received a card and it came from the Fichtelgebirge in Germany. Picture postcards, with forest scenes and theatre halls, continued to arrive at regular intervals. Letters were rare, and they never mentioned the gruelling training with a single word.

Only a year later, when father received a furlough, he told us how he had travelled to Germany. At the railway station in Temeswar, the men were gathered in a large room. A spokesman once again reminded them of their duty as German men, to fight for Germany in this struggle for existence. He also enumerated all the advantage of serving in the German army. In the end, almost all the men in the room opted for the German army. They were then led to a railway car, which was sealed as a foreign cargo and brought them directly to Vienna.

The arrival in Vienna turned out to be a tremendous surprise for the men from the Banat. Right at the station they were insulted by the workers employed there as prolongers of the war. On a car someone had written in chalk: "The ethnic German monkeys are Hitler's secret weapons". After this reception, there was not a single man in the group, who did not wish that he could return home. Unfortunately, they were part of a huge machine and could no longer act as they pleased.

Soon the vast majority of the young men from the village had gone to Germany. The talk in the village was about the Grafenwöhr training camp, about the incredible efforts and near-starvation during the training period. In their first letters home from the battle front, their location was not given. The relatives were told, however, that the units to which the men of the village had been assigned, was at first fighting in Yugoslavia and later in Russia.

Principal Bachus was among the first to go to war and a young teacher stood before our class every day. Dr. Wetzler was also missing from the village. It was said that he had certified all the men of the village as fit for military service in the German army and had signed the necessary papers. Many villagers could not forgive him that he had made no difference between the healthy and the sick.

Soon the news reached the village of the villagers killed in action. Almost every week there was a requiem in the church for a fallen son of the village, sometimes even several in the same week. In the daily newspaper there were many black-framed messages, with an Iron Cross, a name, date of birth, and the remark that they had died for the fatherland. Was this fatherland Romania? Or was it Germany? Or was it the Banat? The whole Banat or only the fragment allocated to Romania? Did it really matter, when so many young lives were cut short?

Many women did men's work, and the worry about their husbands and sons was written in their faces. One day in front of the milk-collection station of the cooperative appeared the so-called striker box. My way to school each day led me past this advertizing station. Under glass there were photos and articles, some of which I had already seen in the magazine "Signal". At the bottom of the wooden cage was a white-painted board with the inscription in black letters: "The Jews are to blame for this war." Who were these Jews? Since there were no Jews in the village, I had not known any of them. I asked Kaspar, where these Jews actually lived and whether they were really that bad. His answer was: "Some Jews are good; others are bad, as is the case with any larger group of people anywhere".

Then he told me the story of the storekeeper Welsch. A few years ago he wanted to start selling textile goods in his shop, but did not have the money needed for the initial purchase of the textiles. He traveled to Temeswar and visited a number of big textile stores, of which he knew that they were owned by German merchants. To get the textiles, all of them demanded either cash or a written guarantee signed by at least one person known to be reliable. As Welsch could produce neither one nor the other, he could not get the fabric and had to go home with empty hands. On his way to the railway station, he passed a large Jewish textile store. Since he had nothing to lose, he went in the store and presented his case to the owner. The owner listened attentively and then said, "Choose what you need and take it home with you. Once you sold it, you can pay for it and again choose the merchandise you like."

Welsch was surprised and asked, "How can you trust me, when you don't know me, when I have no cash and no guarantor?" The answer was: "I can recognize an honest man when I see one." The encounter resulted in a long-standing relationship, which was very satisfying for both sides and also for the village customers of storekeeper Welsch.

Years later I learned that this story had a sequel. Welsch was in a town of Ukraine, and he also wore a German uniform. He was the oldest in a group of boys from the Banat. Part of the group was resting, while their comrades were unloading some material. Under the supervision of the soldiers, this not exactly easy work was being done by old men from the small town, among them many Jews. A boy from the village was walking behind an old man and drove him on with the words: "Move it, old man, we do not have all day."

He had heard this phrase used by a soldier from Germany and replayed it to impress his peers. Welsch, who was standing nearby, said to the boy: "Hansi, he is also a human being!" Hansi turned red in the face, and from that day on, he treated all detainees and labourers humanely. Unfortunately, he did not survive the following year and his grave is somewhere in Russia, as are the graves of many young villagers.

There was no electricity in the village at the time, but more and more villagers acquired battery-powered radios. Not only Uncle Gerhard, but also our Becker relatives had bought a radio. My mother, Oma and I now spent many an evening at their house listening to radio station Belgrade, operated by the German military. I remember the signature song "Lili Marleen", which never failed to fill the women's eyes with tears. No wonder that the song became the favourite song of the soldiers of the Afrikakorps, and even a favourite of their English opponents in Northern Africa. Later on, the English had to bring out an English version of the song, which is still well known to the war generation in English-speaking countries.

I remember one late summer evening, when several neighbours had gathered at Beckers to listen to an important speech on the radio. The wait must have been too long for me and I must have fallen asleep, because I can not remember anything about the speech. But I do remember that an important person had spoken and the neighbours considered the speech to be of great importance. After the speech was finished, my mother woke me up for the walk home.

I still remember the many excited people on the street. The names of Goebbels and Hitler were mentioned again and again. Kaspar was standing in a group, and he was not in a good mood when he said to the bystanders in a loud voice: "The Russians will come to our village and they will take away all your possessions". The people standing around him did not want to hear that, but most of them had a worried look as they went home.

On a Saturday evening, the hall of the Great Inn was filled with people. The drum man, as the "town crier" was called, had announced a speech to be given by a general of the Wehrmacht, holder of the Iron Cross. It was said that the General had come directly from the battlefront and was going to give the people a better understanding of the current stage of the war. I learned afterwards that he gave a powerful speech, full of examples of bravery in the field and confidence in a victory. He spoke of the bravery of the German soldiers and their brilliant leaders, of new weapons, and of strategic retreats that were only temporary. Very few people drew new hope, and most remained sceptical, including Kaspar and Father Molnar. Kaspar had noticed that the General had read his speech from a printed manuscript, which indicated that it had been prepared by others.

The General was invited for dinner at the house of lumber seller Glass. After dinner the men sat together in the office of Mr. Glass, smoking cigars and drinking brandy. As the evening went on, the mood of the General darkened noticeably. Much as he tried, he could not suppress his tears. In the end he broke down and said under the flowing tears: "The poor boys, they were the best. They are all dead, killed for nothing . . . for nothing"

The general gloom in the village could not remain hidden to us children. Lumber dealer Glass was now convinced that the time had come for him to prepare for the unavoidable refuge to the West. The next day he began very quietly to cover his wagon and load it up with the provisions necessary for the long journey. He was determined to stay ahead of the Red Army that was in the process of overrunning Europe.

# 8.  THE LAST FURLOUGH

In school, the new teacher continued with her program, despite all the rumours and ramblings. We learned our reading, writing and arithmetic, we had assemblies in the schoolyard, and we sang old folk songs and new marching songs. One day a woman coming from the railway station passed our school, and mentioned that my father is among the just-arrived soldiers. Given such an occasion, I was allowed to leave for home immediately. I ran home and found my mother calmly sitting in the garden in front of a pile of potatoes, which she had just awakened from hibernation. We run more than we walked down the street leading to the train station. We met my father in front of the Beckers house, surrounded by a dozen people, among them Mrs. Gilde and Mrs. Kremling. All of them were waiting for some good news from the front and were clearly disappointed when my father had not brought them. For our family it was a happy reunion in this uncertain time, even with the uncertainty and fear always lurking in the background.

After many conversations back and forth, my mother promised solemnly that we will use any opportunity to flee to the West whenever it was certain that the Russians will reach the Banat and our village. There was much cooking and baking going on in our house, and there was no end of visitors.

The day before father had to leave, my parents stood in the garden, with their arms intertwined, as if nothing could separate them from each other. They tried to hide their tears from me, but did not succeed. Oma was in the house, quietly crying to herself. There was a feeling that no one knew who would survive this war or what it will leave of our family. Every one tried to console the others by reminding them that the neighbours, relatives and acquaintances were all in the same position. Everyone had to try to get by somehow, to survive the war. As far anybody knew, every war had ended and for the survivors, life eventually returned to normal. Why should it be different this time?

The night before the early morning departure of my father, I wanted to accompany him and my mother to the train station. They promised to wake me up, but it was very early and they let me sleep. When I woke up and saw the teary eyes of the women, I did not have to look at the clock to know that my father had already left. Whether and when we would see him again, and after how many months or years, was as uncertain as our whole of life in those days.

Eventually Romanian refugees came to the village. It was said that they were either from Bessarabia or Bukovina, both of which had already been overrun by the Red Army. The absence of men in the village had led to a shortage of labour, and so the refugees willing to work found work and living quarters in the village. Village locksmith Roos had hired a helper, but claimed that he was very lazy and hardly useful. After serious arguments between the two men, the helper threatened Roos that he would have him shot by the Russians, as soon as they came to the village.

In those days of September, when village leader Wirth was already fighting on the Eastern Front, his superior, the district leader, came to the village. Mother went to listen to his speech in front of the town hall and came home somewhat reassured. A temporary evacuation of the village had been ordered by higher authorities. Lists would be created and then the necessary railway wagons would be provided, so that those willing to take refuge in the West could be evacuated properly. But the days went by and nothing happened. Rumours spread in the village about violence by Soviet soldiers. Uncle Gerhard explained to anyone who would listen that these rumours were merely inventions of propaganda. In some yards, covered wagons could be seen, prepared to take the families to the West. Many farmers, who had a horse and cart, or tractor and wagon, made their own preparations for the escape. Since we had no horse or cart, we had to wait on the promised rail cars. This caused my mother much worry, but she would not ask anyone to take us with them. To get out of this predicament, there was only one rule: every man has to look out for himself.

Quite unexpectedly, a unit of the Hungarian army arrived in the village. The Hungarian soldiers told the people that the Banat had been returned to Hungary and started changing Romanian Lei into Hungarian Pengö. The soldiers gave me some coins to enrich my small coin collection. They also filled my father's workshop with straw and about ten of them spent the night there. On the main street they had placed some guns in position, with their barrels pointing in the direction of Temeswar. The war seemed to approach our village from Temeswar. We boys could not believe that the war that had been raging in far away Russia was now in the vicinity of our peaceful village.

When the morning dawned, the Hungarian soldiers had left as quietly as they had arrived. Neighbour Maria told mother that the village policeman had also left the village. A passer-by said that the Russians were already in Temeswar. An eerie, ominous silence lay over the village like the beginning of a nightmare. The anxious anticipation of what was going to happen next had captured every villager.

During the short period that the Ethnic Group had been running the village, every house in the village was obliged to hoist the Romanian flag and the German flag on Romanian and German national holidays and similar occasions. As a consequence, there was a German flag with the swastika in each house. As the Russians drew closer, people would ask themselves what to do with this flag. The pessimists were the majority in the village; they just threw the swastika-flag in the oven. Others, including our neighbour Maria, believed that the retreat of the Germans was only temporary, as described by the district leader of the Ethnic Group. Maria opened up the cover of an upholstered chair, put the folded flag inside, and sewed it back on.

Neighbour Hekler found a more practical approach: his wife just separated the white, round centre piece from the flag, creating a simple red flag. Although there was no hammer and sickle, it could be considered an acceptable substitute for a Soviet flag. When the arrival of the Red Army appeared imminent, Hekler asked his son to place the flag on the gable of their house. The young Hekler had always had enemies in the village, ever since he was excused from service in both the Romanian and German army. One evening he was on his way home with his horse and cart, from some work in his fields, when suddenly several young men jumped on his car, dragged him down and beat him mercilessly. His father found him later in the evening, covered with blood and lying in the ditch. The red flag still hang on their house, but in these turbulent days, neither friend nor enemy paid any attention to it.

# 9.  THE RED ARMY IN OUR VILLAGE

The streets were empty and the village looked deserted in the late September sun. No man, no chicken, not even a dog could be seen. Oma, mother and I were down on our knees in front of the bedroom window, which allowed a free view of the closest street intersection. A cart like all the other peasant carts in the village appeared, pushed by five or six men. The men wore dirty uniforms and looked pretty scruffy. They were the first soldiers of the Red Army, simply called "the Russians" by most of us, our "liberators" and new masters.

Later that day, two Russians appeared in our yard and asked for two chickens. Grandma helped them catch two chickens and they left. They went on to Maria's house, where they also took two chickens. Mother did not come out of the house, but I was not afraid. The adults were generally more afraid than the children. We had all lost our appetites and barely touched our dinner. Maria joined us, but she came through the back yard and garden; she was afraid to go out on the street. The women talked excitedly to each other, especially when I was not around them.

Mother and Oma took turns for the night watch, but I had a restless sleep, with nightmares that awoke me a few times. In the morning we saw several Russian soldiers on the street in front of our house, all moving towards the pasture located on the village side closest to Neusiedel. Around noon we heard the first rifle shots. We were again looking through the window to the street-side of the house, watching our neighbour Mr. Lux, the husband of the older Maria. He stood behind a big old mulberry tree and seemed in conversation with the neighbour on the other side of the street, whose head stuck out through an open window.

We opened our window and heard the repeated closing remark by Mr. Lux: "These are all just warning shots." Astonishing was that he was not speaking the local dialect, but Standard German. He had obviously had a few drinks, perhaps for a little extra courage. We noticed that he stood on the proper side of the tree, the one opposite Neusiedel. That was definitely the right thing to do, because the shots clearly came from the direction of Neusiedel.

In the afternoon the gunfire became louder and more intense. There was clearly artillery fire mixed in with the fire of rifles and machine guns. We were scared in our own home and went through the backyard and garden to our neighbours. Mr. Lux was sober now, and agreed with the rest of us that these were not warning shots, and what was happening was more than a manoeuvre. On the opposite side of our street we saw some Russians who came back from their positions on the meadow at the railway embankment. An officer was wearing a white bandage under his officer's cap.

A woman neighbour came over in great panic and said that the secondary building of Toni Schwarz had been set on fire by an artillery shot. That explained the smoke and the smell of burning, both of which were driven by the wind towards our neighbourhood. We had visited that family just a few days earlier, when their son Peter had been home on leave from the front.

Late in the afternoon the shooting suddenly stopped. A group of people run more than walked past our house. They were on their way from their houses near the meadow, to the opposite side of the village. We joined them and reached the house of the Klemens family, just as the shooting began again. Mr. Klemens invited us to spend the night in their basement. He explained that it had a ceiling made of reinforced concrete, and therefore was as safe as possible. It turned out to be the first night in my life that I spend in a cellar. I still was not afraid and felt safe in the presence of mother and Oma. Moreover, there were more than a dozen people with us in that cellar.

Towards evening, when the shooting subsided again, mother decided to go back to our house, mainly to feed the pigs, chickens and rabbits, and also to get some blankets to make our beds for the night in the basement. While she was on the way back, after she had just crossed the main street, the shooting started again. Several artillery shells hit the ground near her, and every time she had to throw herself on the ground. She ended up with a small splinter wound in the leg, on which Mr. Klemens immediately placed a proper bandage. Oma was terrified that mother had risked her life, but was happy at the same time that mother escaped with her life and without major wounds.

The morning began with more shooting, but it sounded as if the shots were fired right in front of the basement door. The basement had no toilet and I had to use a pause in the firing to step out. Suddenly a panicky fear grabbed me and I ran as fast as I could back to the safety of the basement.

Around noon, there was silence in the village when all weapons stopped firing. The silence felt good and one could almost believe the whole war episode was over. Mother, Oma and I thanked the Klemens family and made our way up the street, to the Quintus family. We were related to them and they had a large and modern wine cellar, which could certainly withstand some artillery shots. On the road, we suddenly saw three soldiers, all with camouflage uniforms and black faces. They carried a machine gun and several cases of ammunition. We turned to run away, but they called to us in German. They told us that the village was now in German hands and that we had nothing more to fear. We were happy to tell old Mr. Quintus and his wife, that the Germans were here now, and the Russians had left the village. Could the temporary Soviet occupation of our village really be over?

# 10. Escape to the neighbouring village

The next morning the news spread from cellar to cellar, that the German occupation troops had ordered the civilians to leave the village. The sun was high in the sky when we made our way back home, to our house. Near the house of the Roth family, we crossed the main street and found to our horror that there were two dead bodies spread on the ground. The two villagers had been killed by shrapnel, not far from the place where my mother had ended up with a splinter wound two days ago. People were in a rush to leave the village and no one cared for the bodies.

Once in our house, we packed up some things, fed the pigs, chickens and rabbits and joined the column of people moving down the street in the direction of Neusiedel. Mother pushed the bike next to her. It was packed with our belongings that hang down from both sides of the bike. Neusiedel was occupied by German troops, who seemed not to pay any attention to us refugees. Before entering the village, we admired their artillery, in position on the left side of the road.

In Bogarosch, the Denoel family did not hesitate to take us in. They were our relatives, but only grandma knew the exact degree of kinship. Also at the Denoel were Uncle Gerhard, Mrs. Gilde and her children Hilde and Hermann, whom I had always called "my Gilde cousins". Then Mrs. Kremling joined us, together with her son Robert and daughter Simone. It was just our luck that the Denoel family had a large village house in which there was room for all of us. There was a room for the three boys, while the girls remained with their parents. On Saturday Hermann, Robert and I worked the pump to move rain water from an underground reservoir into a barrel installed in the attic. Meanwhile the women were firing up the water heater in the bathroom. First, the girls took a bath, followed by boys, and finally by the adults. We boys often admired the Denoel's two strong horses and the impressive tractor which displayed the name of its producer on both of its sides: Hanomag.

During the following week my mother tried to go back to our village at least every other day. She usually made the short trip with neighbours who owned a horse and cart. Almost everyone had animals to feed and everybody wanted to keep an eye on his house. Not all Germans had left the village and it seemed that all Romanian refugees had remained in the village. It became apparent that some of those left behind in the village spent their time doing mischief. When mother returned to our house for the first time, she was startled: Someone had broken in through the front door, had rummaged through our belongings, bits and pieces of which were strewn all over the floor. The large wall clock, the pride of my father, stood on the table in the middle of the room, its door was open, the pendulum swung back and forth, but the clock showed the exact time, as always. Mother wrapped the clock in a blanket and brought it to Bogarosch.

Mother tried to coerce our dog along, but the animal stubbornly refused to come along. During each visit, she left enough food for several days for the pigs, rabbits and chickens, and she chose a few things to bring to Bogarosch. We had two burlap sacks packed with the most important of our belongings, in preparation for the flight to Germany. Just like in Alexanderhausen, a list of the families willing to flee had been set up in Bogarosch, again with the promise that there would be rail cars for all. When nothing came of this promise, my mother was deeply shaken and often close to tears. Even greater was her despair, when Mrs. Kremling at the last moment found an opportunity to escape: a distantly related family from her native village invited her and her children to join them in their covered horse cart.

The funeral of six German soldiers lives on in my memory. The soldiers had lost their lives near Pesak. Among the many villagers from Bogarosch who had shown up at the cemetery, there were many of us boys. It was a moving celebration for all. After the honour guard fired its salvo in the air, some boys jumped to collect the shell casings. I waited until the honour guard withdrew, before collecting a shell casing. This casing became an important object of my collection of war souvenirs.

Locksmith Roos had remained in the village, perhaps because he had a plan and was determined to carry it out. One day he treated two young soldiers to a lunch with abundant brandy, the type we called raki.

After lunch they all went into the village and searched for the Romanian refugee who had been the helper of master Roos. It is said that they found him in the Rondell, sentenced him to death by firing squad, placed him against a tree and carried out the verdict. When Roos awoke from his drunkenness, he was appalled by what happened. He tried to displace the event from his memory, but was unsuccessful. He could only go on living by reminding himself over and over, that it was just the unspeakable war, and if somebody had to die, then better the refugee rather than Roos.

Our neighbour, Mr. Lux, was on his way back from Alexanderhausen to Bogarosch, when once again the artillery fire started. He stopped at a makeshift bomb shelter in Neusiedel, where the family of principal Bachus had also taken shelter. The teacher's wife, her mother and a baby were all huddled together. Mrs. Bachus complained bitterly about the hopeless situation of the villagers, and from which they could see no way out. Then her mother said: "Only God can help us get out of our misery."

The principal's wife replied: "No God can help us anymore. Only Adolf Hitler can still help us." When it appeared to get a little quieter outside, neighbour Lux said goodbye, stepped outside and started walking in the direction of Bogarosch. He had barely reached the end of the street, when a direct hit from the Russian artillery struck the shelter. There were no survivors, but the number of civilian dead from our village had now risen to seventeen. Neighbour Lux was prepared throughout his life to swear any oath to the fact that his report was the pure, unadulterated truth.

After nearly two rainy weeks, the sun finally showed its face to Bogarosch. Mr. Denoel hitched his horses to a cart and we went to his vineyard. We searched for ripe grapes and found some. In the east, our village could be seen and we suddenly noticed that several smoke plumes stood above the houses. Judging by the number of plumes, there had to be at least a dozen homes on fire. Mr. Denoel drove back home at top speed. There was Uncle Gerhard sitting in front of his radio and told us with a smile on his face: "Radio Moscow just announced in the news that the glorious Red Army has just begun an offensive northwest of Temeswar."

We could hear that the shooting was approaching Bogarosch, so we all moved in the cellar of the house. It did not take a long time before the Russians rushed into Bogarosch, with loud shouts of "Urra". The Germans offered no resistance; they seemed to have left the village already. We spent another night in the basement, in anxious expectation of the events that were to follow.

In the morning, the younger women put on the clothes of the older ones and each one tried to make herself look as repulsive as possible. Around noon, a not exactly young-looking Russian showed up and indicated by gestures that he was hungry and wanted something to eat. He seemed to also pay attention to the women. Mrs. Denoel brought bacon and bread, while Uncle Gerhard found somewhere a bottle of brandy. That was a big mistake because as the drinking went on, the Russian was getting louder and louder. All of us gradually managed to hide in the cellar again, leaving our Uncle Gerhard to entertain the guest. When the Soviet soldier later went in the yard and fired his submachine gun into the air, we climbed through a basement window, one after another, into the neighbouring yard, and from there we ran through the gardens to the Denoel relatives who lived at the other end of the village. There we spent the night and in the morning we returned cautiously to the Denoel house. We learned that later on Uncle Gerhard had to leave the house, leaving the Russian in charge of the house and everything in it.

Uncle Gerhard was greatly embarrassed when he told us what had happened next. When the Russian had enough of eating and drinking, he looked at Uncle Gerhard's shirt and found that he liked it. He asked Gerhard with unmistakable gestures to take it off and give it to him. Then he asked for clean underwear, and when Gerhard indicated that he could not find any, he threw him out into the yard, followed by a jar of honey from one of our burlap sacks.

Uncle Gerhard, now afraid for his life, found a way to leave the house. He remained in the neighbourhood, as he felt responsible for the consequences of his absence. When the Russians finally left the house, Gerhard immediately returned there. The first attempt at fraternization had failed, and he promised himself to refrain from any further attempts.

A few days later, we thanked the Denoel family for their hospitality and returned to Alexanderhausen. Our front door was open, because the broken lock had not been repaired. The pigs ran around in the backyard and garden, but mother was able lure them back to their barn with some food. I was able to catch four of my five rabbits. The great pendulum clock received a new place on the wall, this time in the room where the three of us were now living. We had given the chamber to a woman whose house had burned down during the battle.

Most of the houses destroyed by fire were located on the south-western edge of the village, facing the meadow toward Neusiedel. The German army had withdrawn in that direction and some speculated that the smoke was meant to cover their retreat. When he had left the village, Uncle Gerhard had hired Vetter Jakob to stay in the village and look after his large house. When he returned from Bogarosch and stepped into his house, Gerhard found a large burn mark in the middle of a room. Jakob told him a compelling story: The previous day, like every day before, he went to Gerhard's house, to see what was happening. When he entered the house, he found in the middle of the big room a burning pile of papers that had come out of a drawer. He could not see who had scattered the papers on the floor, or who had set them on fire. He immediately threw his jacket on the papers and extinguished the fire, thus saving the house from burning down.

In gratitude for saving his great house, Uncle Gerhard gave Jacob as a present a smaller house that he also owned in the village. Many people were surprised that the other three houses located at this intersection of two streets had actually burned down. But no one could know at the time that all the houses were soon to pass in the possession of the state.

On the main street, only two houses had fallen victim to the fire: the house of the rich farmer Spanagel and the house of the storekeeper Lorenz. Both houses were neighbours of the house inhabited by Mr. and Mrs. Tines. One was adjacent to the Tines's house and the other was located just across Main Street. The Spanagel family had fled, but some neighbours and other villagers suspected that Tines had something to do with the fire at the two houses. But they had no evidence so they could never express their presumptions publicly.

Two streets away from our house lived the family Mayer. The Mayers had also found refuge in Bogarosch. Mayer still had a so called "Russian horse", a smaller horse left behind by the Russians, after they had taken his two big horses. When he returned from Bogarosch one day, he found that the Russians had used his large summer kitchen as a medical station. In addition to all kinds of materials, there were also four corpses, and they were no longer in a good condition. To make the house habitable again, he first had to get rid the bodies. But he could not do that alone and no other help was available. Adjacent to his garden was a long garden, which currently had no real owner. The legal owner had been in America for many years, and the garden was planted with corn by a distant relative of the owner, when it was not sitting there empty and uncultivated. With a shovel, Mayer dug a deep pit in the garden next door. Then he attached a rope to the harness of his "Russian horse" and dragged the bodies into the pit, one by one. He did so reluctantly and he had to overcome a lot of nerves, but he persevered because he had to make the house habitable, so that his family could move back in.

The returnees soon found out that the village had changed once again. The ruins of the burned-down homes stood out in the village like unhealed wounds. The deserted homes of villagers who had fled to the West were empty and were taken over by Romanian colonists. The colonists were often the same Romanians who in earlier years had passed through the village with their covered wagons, selling their apples. Mother, Oma and I now lived in our large room, the room with the four windows. I had taken over grandfather's bed, while mother slept on the sofa, a visible sign that the arrangement was regarded as temporary. Actually, the whole village life felt like it was makeshift or temporary. The villagers were glad to be alive, but one lived only from one day to another.

On a sunny fall day mother and I pulled our little cart up to our potato field near the "Uiheler road", which was the street leading to Neusiedel. We wanted to provide our shrunk household with potatoes for the winter. Suddenly a Russian biplane landed on the meadow, and I wondered how the Red Army could win the war with this type of aircraft. The pilot took out a map and confirmed his location with one of the many bystanders that had appeared out of nowhere. Then he started his engine and flew off toward the east.

Soon the mulberry trees lost their leaves and winter slowly took over from autumn. At Christmas, mother baked a cake with several layers of dough and with a caramel filling. Where she had found the sugar was her secret, as all stores were closed. The mood of my mother had lightened a little, she cried only when she felt unobserved. No one wanted to say it out loud, but the question of whether my father was still alive and where he may be weighed heavily on her and preoccupied us all.

# 11.  Deportation to the USSR

- My mother - Barbara Tullius, née Lukas

The year 1945 started with a snow-less January, but winter was in the air, when the village crier announced his orders: All men between 17 and 45 and women between 18 and 35 years had to present themselves in the hall of the Great Inn, bringing with them enough food for two weeks. Since the purpose of this order was not specifically stated, many of those affected assumed that they were needed for some work that needed to be completed within two weeks, somewhere in the region. Since it was winter, and winter is not the season for work in agriculture, it was rumoured that our people were destined for forced labour in the Soviet Union. Contributing to this rumour was an eerie experience of some women from Alexanderhausen: They had seen a most unusual train at the railway station in Temeswar. Its cattle cars were filled with people who identified themselves as Swabians from Yugoslavia. They said that they were on their way to forced labour in Russia. A woman from one of the cattle cars had shouted: "Watch out, you will be next!"

Mother and neighbour Maria the younger had hidden in the straw stack of the burnt-down Becker house. The next day we had a visit from a policeman and a girl from the village. They had a list of names which included the name of my mother. They told us that my mother must come forward because she must do her duty like everybody else. Oma said that mother was born in America, she was an American citizen, and therefore did not belong to the list. The visitors were not prepared to deal with this situation and moved on. They came back on the following day and wanted to see an American passport or birth certificate. Grandma said that we did not have these documents in our possession, but would have to request them from the U.S.A. The policeman shook his head and said that he was not prepared to wait. My mother should join the group, or he would take Oma instead, until mother showed up.

After another cold night in the straw stack, my mother and young Maria decided to come out of hiding and join the others. Refusing to appear seemed to them a dishonest choice. If all their peers had to do their duty, they had an obligation to do the same. They saw themselves as members of a community in which they did not want to be the exceptions. They packed the necessary food and joined the assembled group in the Great Inn. Of the assembled men and women, many still believed that they would be away only for a short labour assignment. Others were convinced that they were destined to be taken to Russia. They all lived their final days in their home village with a sense of uncertainty and insecurity.

After accompanying mother to the collection point, Oma returned with tearful eyes. Then she sat down at the table and wrote a letter to her sister in Cincinnati. In it, she implored her sister to send us the birth certificate of my mother, as soon as possible. Although the prospects for success were very bad, that birth certificate was her last hope.

On one of the following mornings, the villagers detained at the Great Inn were marched off to Perjamosch. They were accompanied by Romanian gendarmes and soldiers with fixed bayonets. The detainees from some of the neighbouring villages had also been brought to Perjamosch, where they were herded into a large school. There they would be placed in cattle cars for the trip into the unknown. None of them knew when the journey was to begin, what its destination would be, and most importantly, why this was done to our innocent young people.

A day or two after the departure of our young people, Oma and I made our way to Perjamosch, carrying food and some clothing for my mother. We could only speak and shake hands with my mother through the iron grating that was on top of the school wall and is probably still there today. Mother tried to be as confident as she possibly could. She stressed that this also will pass and that we should all take good care of ourselves until we were reunited again. We said goodbye and turned to go home. Suddenly, I was struck by a thought: "You are now seeing your mother for the last time!" I turned around and stood like petrified. My eyes searched for my mother. She stood still on the same spot and waved from the other side of the iron fence. I thought I could see her tears. Finally, Oma placed her hand on my shoulders and said quietly: "Come, my child, we have to go home."

On the long way home I could not shake the thought that I had seen my mother for the last time. My eyes filled with tears again and again. I knew that Oma could see it, but I was not embarrassed, because she also kept wiping the tears from her eyes. It was dark when we arrived at our house, two totally shaken people, and it was good that it was dark, so that no one could see the tears of the other.

When the next day dawned, the air smelled of snow, but Oma told me that she needed to take more clothes for mother to Perjamosch. She set out on the road, in the hope that she would get a lift in a horse-drawn cart, since many would be on the road to Perjamosch. The first snow fell even before she had left the village. Not a single car was on the road and she walked all the way to Perjamosch. Mother was very happy with the additional winter clothes that Oma had brought her. But she was concerned about how Grandma would walk back home through all that snow. When the two women parted, there were many more tears.

When Oma started out on her way home, the wind-whipped snow was so thick that she could barely see three steps ahead. Once again, no horse cart could be seen on the street that could have taken her home to the village. When she reached the Szeged highway, it was deserted and the layer of snow was steadily getting thicker. As she approached the

Pakatz Puszta, the wind had reached the power of a full-scale storm. She wrapped her scarf around her head and shoulders, but could feel the icy wind getting through all her clothing. The snow was still getting deeper and she could feel the weariness overtake her. Suddenly she slipped and fell on the road. She tried to get up, but the pain in her right foot made it impossible. After several unsuccessful attempts, she knew that she could not get up without help. She recalled later that she prayed for help, while her consciousness drifted into a dreamlike state.

The old Nowak, as he was called in the village, was on his way home from Perjamosch, travelling through the snow with his horse-drawn cart. He was letting his horse move at whatever speed it wanted, while his thoughts were on the uncertain fate of his daughter, to whom he had just said goodbye in Perjamosch. He was already several cart lengths past it, when he thought that he had noticed an unusual hill in the snow. He stopped, dismounted and went back. Under that barely noticeable mount of snow he found Oma. He could not understand what she murmured in reply to his questions. He just grabbed her and carried her to his cart. He put her down in the back of the cart and covered her with a horse blanket. Then he drove home as fast as he could. His wife made a camomile tea and Oma slowly revived. Nothing was frozen, but her right foot was swollen and she could not stand on it.

Meanwhile I sat at home all alone and waited. As the evening approached and the storm raged on, my concern turned into fear. I put on my winter coat and went to the Becker's house. Mrs. Becker had just come back from the Nowak's and told me briefly about the accident. That same evening the Beckers and old Nowak brought Oma home with the horse cart. Joining their hands together, they carried her in the house, and put her in her bed, which she could not leave for six weeks. There was no doctor in our village or in any of the neighbouring villages. Eventually a medic came to the house, but he could not determine whether the foot was broken or just sprained. There were no medications to be had anywhere and Oma had to live with the continuing pain, day after day, night after night. Mrs. Becker and sometimes Mr. Becker himself came to our house every morning to get the great room-heater going. They always brought us something to eat, sometimes even two or three times a day. "We were lucky once again, even with all that went wrong!" Mrs. Becker told me.

As the sun became stronger, Oma's condition gradually improved. She said every day that she wanted nothing more than to get up and do her work. Soon she could stay up for longer periods and even prepare our meals. I helped her as best I could. Over time, the foot healed, but something was not quite right with it. After a long search we finally found a doctor. He came to the conclusion that the foot had not healed in its normal position. He would have to break it again and then set it to heal properly. Oma wanted no part of that, and preferred to limp through all her remaining years. Fortunately for both of us, she was able to keep her sewing machine in motion with her healthy foot, throughout the days and often into the night. Through this work she kept what was left of our family alive for many years to come.

Among the rounded-up villagers locked up in the secondary school of Perjamosch was Franz Tines. He spent his days and nights thinking about an escape plan. On the day of departure, he was very slow packing his backpack and let the guards know several times that he had a severe stomach ache. After most of the prisoners had left the room, he played his trump card. From his pocket he took a superb gold watch with a thick gold chain. He opened the lid on it and waved it in front of the soldier guarding him. With words and gestures he made it clear to the soldier that he very, very urgently needed to go to the toilet. He handed the soldier his watch and chain and asked him to hold it until he returned from the toilet. The soldier looked around, and since no one was around except for the two of them, he took the watch and let Tines run in the direction of the toilets.

During the previous days, Tines had studied the building in detail. He ran past the toilets to the stairs leading to the attic, climbed up there and lay down in its farthest corner. He remained there until he heard the whistle of the locomotive and the train began to move out. No one came looking for him. He waited a few minutes before he climbed cautiously down the stairs. The school was empty and abandoned; there was no sign of troops or militiamen. He crept along the alley that leads towards the village of Pesak. If he heard the slightest sound, he stood still behind a tree or lay down on the ground. He left Perjamosch behind and walked in the middle of the empty country road, in the direction of Pesak.

It was a cold night, but he hardly felt the cold. He was likely to catch a cold, but he kept telling himself that he had escaped from certain death. He went around Pesak as best he could, because he knew the area from previous visits. Once he was scared by some dogs, but he came through unobserved. The Szeged highway was empty. He had to walk in the middle of the road where the snow was less deep. When he reached the village, he could notice the break of day. He crept along the houses and came to the familiar garden wall of his neighbour. He climbed over the wall into the garden, which adjoined his own garden. When he knocked gently at the window of his own house, his wife was so terrified that she could not utter a sound. He fell on his bed dead tired, but his wife thought that she could still see a smile on his face.

# 12. POST-WAR UNCERTAINTY

The following months had something unreal about them. The village had become unreliable and unpredictable. Even we, the children felt the insecurity, because so many of the adults were missing, and the village did no longer feel intact. So many adult relatives and neighbours were not there any more. And there were too many strangers around us. A store had burnt down during the battle and all the others were closed. The butcher's store was also closed, but word got around when somebody had killed a calf or a cow in the village or in a neighbouring village. The money had lost his value and the barter system arose again, like in the dawn of history.

Nobody knew exactly who had survived and who had died, where the survivors had found shelter, or where the dead were buried. The people had become the toys of fate; all human life had lost his value. Slowly, everybody got to know which houses were unoccupied and closed because their owners had managed to escape to the west. Those deported to Russia had disappeared from the surface of the earth: No letter, no postcard, no sign of life came from them.

My friend Richard had also managed to escape to the west with his grandparents. At the beginning, his absence made me feel sad, but at the same time I was glad that he did not have to live through our misfortunes. Kaspar had disappeared; nobody knew whether he had been deported to Russia, or had fled to Germany.

One day we received a postcard addressed to my mother and it came from my father. He had survived the war and was in Germany, in an English camp for prisoners of war. The card was a sign of life, but not much more. We were very happy that he had survived. If we would only receive a similar postcard from my mother, our happiness would be complete. But nothing arrived from Russia. The whole village was waiting for even the slightest sign of life from the deported, but no such sign came. If they were still alive, why would not one of them write a postcard? Could they all have been killed? The villagers asked those questions of one another, but nobody had an answer. The families of the abductees were overwhelmed by worry. Somebody out there wanted us to suffer, only we did not know who and we did not know why.

Soviet troops moved through the village again and again, on their way to Hungary. The front was apparently bogged down and on some days the rumble of artillery seemed to come closer to us. On one of those days, four Russians were billeted with us. They made themselves comfortable in the kitchen and asked Oma in a friendly and nonthreatening sign language, whether she would cook something for them. She fried some bacon for them, and they were very grateful. During the night the soldiers slept on the kitchen floor, while Grandma and I slept in our beds in our large room. Only the bolted door between our room and the kitchen separated us from the Russians. We tried to reassure each other that the soldiers were regular people and that they would not do anything to us. The night passed peacefully, but Grandma told me afterwards that she had scarcely closed an eye. The soldiers moved on in the morning, after they had once again thanked Oma for her hospitality. One of them even wanted to pay for the food, but Oma did not accept the unfamiliar money.

There was great astonishment and much head-shaking when some of our refugees to the West returned to the village. They told us about their hunger pains in the camps in Austria and about the farms where they were not welcome. When a Romanian Repatriation Commission promised them that they would get back their houses, their lands and their possessions, several families decided to come back. In the village, they were surprised that their homes were occupied by colonists. They were shocked when they found out that their land had been confiscated. Most returnees had to stay with relatives, neighbours or friends. Now that they were here, they were treated by the authorities just like the ones that had stayed home. They had all lost their livelihoods and were left with nothing except their capability to work, a cheap commodity, ready to be exploited.

Whenever they met, the villagers complained about their horrible situation, because there was no authority that would listen to any complaints concerning their treatment. The returnees from Austria told anybody who would listen, about how bitterly they regretted their return. The difference between the Banat they had left and the Banat to which they had returned, was shocking. They realized that they had fallen victims of mendacious propaganda. All they could do now was to hope for a future opportunity to leave their homeland again. It was a faint hope, but it kept many from utter despair. This is how new plans to emigrate from the Banat germinated.

Despite all that, my surprise and joy were great when my friend Richard came through the door of our house. He had returned home with his grandparents and was very pleased that we were together again. On the large map hanging from our wall, he showed me the locations of Melk and St. Pölten is in Austria. From there, the family had started on their return trip to the Banat. Now they had to repair the part of their house that had not burned down during last fall's battle, to make it habitable and move in.

Some of the men who had been in the German military also returned to the village. In the beginning no one knew exactly how many were home, because they were hiding in their own village. When they had been released from the POW camps, they did what seemed most natural to them: They made an all out effort to return to their village. This is how it was done at all times in living memory: When the war was over, the disarmed soldiers returned to their homes and resumed the thread of their life where the war had broken it. They could not imagine why it would be different this time around.

The journey home was often very dangerous, as it involved long marches on foot and dangerous border crossings. The biggest surprises awaited these returnees at home. Many found that their wives had been deported to Russia. The new rulers regarded the returnees as threats to their state. The returnees could not understand the reason for their persecution. Some of them were unaware of the deportation to the Soviet Union and found out about it for the first time. The deportation took place when the war was still going on, but now the war had ended. They expected to return to their families, to their homes and to their fields. They wanted to continue the only life they knew. They were very willing to contribute to the rebuilding of the country. Why were they chased by the police, arrested and imprisoned, in their own village? How could they be unwanted and persecuted in the land of their birth? They had to find out the hard way that new conditions had been created in the country, conditions that could not be compared to anything previously known.

There was a rumour in the village that neighbour Wirth had returned and was hiding in his house. Nobody, not even the colonists living in his secondary buildings ever saw him, or would admit that they had seen him. In time, however, the militiamen became aware of the rumour and one evening they showed up at Wirths. The women acted surprised and claimed that they knew nothing. The house was examined from the basement to the attic, but they found no trace of Mr. Wirth.

Over time, the militia searched the house a few more times, but always in vain. Years later it was revealed that he spent his days in the basement of his house and in a cave accessible from there. If he was sick, his wife could not even call a doctor. Our neighbour Wirth died in 1947. He was 45 years old and was given a normal burial. The dead could no longer be imprisoned or condemned to the salt mines.

The garden of the Zimmermann family was adjacent to the top of our garden. It had become common knowledge that over many dangerous roads and after many adventures, Hans Zimmermann had come home. Once again the militia learned of it and searched his house on several occasions. One evening I witnessed an unusual scene that reminded me of the stories I had read about the American Wild West. I saw Hans Zimmermann running through the gardens, pursued by two militiamen with drawn guns. I was relieved when the darkness fell and the militiamen had to give up the chase. A few months later, his luck run out and he could not escape. He was captured and taken away with his hands shackled. Soon afterwards it became known throughout the village, that he had been sentenced to work in the coal mines of Anina.

The whole village knew about the adventures of our fellow citizen Nemetz. He was one of the youngest boys enrolled into the Waffen-SS. He also had to overcome a whole course of obstacles to return to Alexanderhausen. He lived with his parents in a small house whose garden was surrounded by a high fence. Every time the militiamen came looking for him, he escaped through one window or another into the backyard of his house or that of one of the neighbouring houses, and disappeared into the gardens. In these gardens he had placed small stones at various places. When the militiamen pursued him, he threw some stones in an arbitrary direction and then lay down flat on the floor. The police officers followed the noise, while Nemetz calmly returned to his house and continued sleeping. Later he is said to have moved the Montan Banat and never returned to his native village.

Meanwhile, the village school had been reopened, with all teaching exclusively in the Romanian language. The new principal, Alexandru, was a Romanian "from Bucharest", which usually meant that he came either from the Bukovina or from Bessarabia. Initially, our class consisted almost entirely of German children, none of whom spoke Romanian. We were supposed to be in the third grade, but we had to start with a Romanian textbook intended for the first grade. At this time there was no talk of any German instruction at all. I still remember vividly, how our class sang a Romanian version of the German folksong "At the well near the gate." It seemed so hilarious that I remember fragments of its text to this day. The total immersion into Romanian, however, had the consequence that we learned the language fairly quickly and fairly thoroughly.

One afternoon in late fall the news electrified our school that some of the villagers that had been deported to Russia had come home. As they were getting off the train, they looked like phantoms and people could not even recognize them. They brought incredible messages from Russia: Many men and women from the village were no longer alive. The most incomprehensible news to me was that my mother was among the dead. I could not accept this message. This simply could not be true; somebody must have made a mistake.

I ran home and saw that the news had already reached Oma, because she was crying loudly as I entered the room. I was surprised that she could believe the incredible, because I could not. When she put her arms around me, I burst out crying loudly. Then Grandma composed herself and said to me: "Now you have no mother and no father. But as long as I live I will always take care of you and be there for you!"

Oma and I visited one of the returnees and what she told us was so incomprehensible and incredible, that I could hardly listen to her story. In the camp at Stalino, my mother stayed healthy until April 1945; she had not even contracted a cold. Then typhus broke out in the camp. Mother was one of the women taken to the infirmary because of suspected infection. Another group of women that included our neighbour Maria visited the infirmary in the evening. The isolated women complained of an unbearable thirst, and begged for water. Mother said she was certainly not ill, but she was very thirsty. Despite the doctor's orders to the contrary, Maria and the other women brought water to the infirmary. The isolated women eagerly drank the water and in the morning their corpses were piled up in front of the infirmary. From there they were taken by horse carriage to some excavated pits, where they were all buried together, while the survivors were completing their shift work as if nothing had happened.

During the following weeks and months I tried long and hard to accept the unbelievable, but I did not succeed. How could my young, mild, innocent mother be driven to her death before her thirtieth birthday? If any justice existed, that could not be possible. Therefore the report had to be a mistake. Every night before going to sleep, I said a silent prayer, as our priest had taught us, and it always ended with the words: "Dear God, let it not be true! Bring us our mother back home safe and sound." But the prayers were not answered, because the dead can not return to the living. After a long time I came to accept that what happened had nothing to do with justice, but only with the absurdity of this unfortunate war.

Romanian colonists continued to arrive in the village. The first had moved in the homes of the Germans who had fled to the West. The later arrivals were housed in the homes of those of us who had stayed behind. The authorities could simply place them in our houses, because these had been officially expropriated and belonged to the state. A woman with a little girl was assigned to our house, the father was to arrive later "from Bucharest". They moved into one of our two large rooms, the one we called the chamber. In addition, they took possession of our summer kitchen located in the secondary building. Their way from the chamber to the summer kitchen was through our kitchen, but we were glad that we did not have to share our kitchen with them. Later they declared themselves satisfied with a quarter of the garden, as well as with the attic of our secondary building.

Just two houses away from us lived the shoemaker Linster and his wife. The two old people were taken in by relatives and the house was taken over by the "wireless operators". These were a small unit of the Romanian military, comprising about ten or twelve soldiers. They built a low wooden tower on the roof of the house and placed an antenna on top of it. Then they erected a second antenna in front of the house, between two tall iron bars. No one knew what their assignment was, or to whom they reported. It was inevitable that I became friends with them and one day I went with them to shoot pigeons.

We had learned that the Pesak Puszta, where no one lived anymore, had become a paradise for pigeons. We went through many uncultivated fields until we reached the dilapidated farm buildings. The pigeons fluttered around everywhere and the radio operators kept shooting until they were out of ammunition. But I felt a strange restlessness. I knew that this was the place where the bodies of the Cherier couple had been found, soon after our return from Bogarosch. The couple had been working the farm on behalf of its owner and lived there, in one of the buildings, during the late summer of 1944. Nobody knew how they had lost their lives or who had killed them. It would always remain a mystery, because no one had ever tried to investigate the murders. Sometimes I thought I could hear the cries of the murdered in the howling of the wind, when it moved through the near-ruins of the Puszta buildings. The radio operators kept talking excitedly and had no idea why I was suddenly so quiet.

It was announced that a Romanian from the Bihar Mountains had been named the new village mayor or reeve. At the beginning he wore home-woven pants and jackets, which were common in his home region. He also wore home-made sandals, made from home-produced leather. His name was Văcaru which means cow herder and many villagers thought the name suited the man. It was established that he could hardly write his name. More important for the village was party secretary Lovitza, a dark-haired, dark-coloured ex-worker, who had come from a city in Old Romania. It was no secret that he had spent some years in a prison. He told anyone who would listen that he had gone to prison because he had been a member of the underground Communist Party of Romania.

The fate of the town and its people had been effectively placed in the hands of these two men. Soon everyone realized that they were only executing the orders of their superiors. They owed their superiors unconditional obedience. No one knew whether these superiors were sitting in Temeswar, or in Bucharest, or even in Moscow. Locally, the two men seemed to have unlimited power over our belongings and even over our daily lives. Many German villagers found it difficult to get used to the idea that these strange and unelected men could exercise absolute power over the village and its inhabitants. But these men only implemented the measures prescribed by their distant masters, and were free to interpret these in whatever way they wanted. Today we know that such actions as the deportation to the USSR were carried out on the direct orders of Stalin. The degree of harshness with which the measures against the German minority were executed, was largely determined by the local rulers. Unfortunately, many of these had just found an outlet to act on their envy and greed.

The expropriation of the houses went on at first without changes visible to the outside world. The Germans remained in their houses, only the houses of those who had escaped to Germany were occupied by colonists. Later, when almost every German family had to share their home with Romanian colonists, the German villagers were already getting used to the fact that they had no rights and must endure whatever harassment the authorities had in store for them. When he first heard about the upcoming expropriation of all means of production, farmer Wambach said: "If anybody is coming to my property to take away my animals and equipment, I will put a knife in his chest." When he met Lovitza, Wambach even tried to convince him that his actions were contrary to established law. Lovitza's answer was: "In this village I am the law!"

When the expropriation commission, accompanied by armed militiamen, later arrived in Wambach's yard, he just remained in the house and let them take whatever they wanted. He had spent his whole life working on the expansion of his agricultural business and each one of his animals was dear to him and each piece of equipment was precious. If they were taken away from him, there would always remain the possibility that he could replace them at a later date. But his life had to be worth more, because he could lose it only once and it could never be replaced.

Time and again new rumours spread in the village and after all they had been put through, the German villagers had to consider that nothing was impossible. They lived in a state of continuing insecurity. All their efforts had to be focused on saving their bare lives. Everything else had become expendable. It was like Uncle Gerhard once aptly said: "If the village crier announced tomorrow that every man has to appear in front of the village hall with a rope around his neck, they will definitely all be there, the poor and the once wealthy, each one with a rope around his neck."

At the beginning the villagers were astonished, how fast an expropriation Commission could be put together. Lovitza and Văcaru just gathered a number of colonists around themselves, those who wanted once again to get some of the Germans' possessions. There was never a shortage of those. How far the powers of the Commission reached, nobody really knew, not even its members. The Commission then went through the streets, from house to house. The self-appointed members of the Commission ransacked the houses and farms of the Germans, and every member took what he wanted.

In our house there were no cows, horses, or farm equipment, just my father's carpentry tools. When we learned that the expropriation Commission was coming down our street, Oma and I hid the carpenter's tools as well as we could, mostly in the darkest corners of the attic. In front of them, we placed half a dozen unfinished coffins, which my father had made for subsequent sales out of stock. When the Commission came to our house, they found only a very heavy workbench and an empty tool cabinet. When some men climbed into the attic and saw the coffins, they crossed themselves and hurried to come back down. The commission went away with empty hands and we thought that we had survived our expropriation well.

Later on, when the Commission was on its way back, the men walked down our street again, one of them suddenly stopped in front of our house, and said: "In there I saw a complete bike". Leader Lovitza apparently had enough for the day and said: "It's getting late, we'll come back tomorrow." At that time, my language skills were already good enough to understand this conversation carried on in Romanian. I knew right away what this was all about: In our barn we had hidden my father's bike inside a pile of unfired bricks.

I went to the barn and saw that the man was right: If you looked carefully, you could see the bike behind the bricks. The next morning I got up early, removed the brick on one side, took out the bike and put the bricks back in their place. Then I pushed the bike into the garden and placed it between some high corn rows. The Commission came back later that day and the men went straight to the unfinished barn. They obviously found no trace of a bicycle. One of them asked us about the bike, but Oma and I just tried to look innocent as we shook our heads. The Commission had to move on empty-handed and the members of the commission could do nothing better than then shake their heads.

The colonist who lived in Beckers' house acquired their cow and offered the Beckers a proposal, which they gladly accepted: "This cow is your cow. You take care of it as before and give me a litre of milk each day. I will also procure the feed." Not far from Becker, the Commission run into a problem. When the Commission entered the courtyard to take their cow away, they found that a woman had chained herself to the door of her cowshed. She was the grandmother of three little girls, whose mother was in Russia and whose father was in Germany. She told the commissioners in German: "First you have to shoot me, before you are taking my only remaining cow away. Then you can feed the three children yourselves." The Commission had never come across such an unusual case. They were perplexed and turned to the Romanian notary for advice. They were told to just leave the old woman and her cow alone.

The next postcard from my father was addressed to Oma. My father had met Uncle Nick in the camp and learned from him that mother had found her death in Russia. It was a devastating blow for father. He simply could not understand how he, who had fought as a soldier in Russia, managed to survive the war, while mother, who was an innocent woman, had been killed. What he was not allowed to write to us at that time was that the men in the POW camp were starving of hunger. Most of the prisoners were just skin and bone, but were not allowed to mention it in their postcards. When the English camp administration asked for volunteers to do farm work in England, many Banaters took up the offer, including my father, Uncle Nick and two more men from Alexanderhausen. One of these men was Hans Cherier, the young son of the couple assassinated on the Puszta Pesak. The second was Dinjer Franz, who had a wife and two children in the village.

On the farms in England, our countrymen were generally treated well. They had enough to eat and they recovered quickly. At first they had to wear uniforms with the inscription "POW" (Prisoner of war) in large letters on the back. They worked hard as they were accustomed to from home and soon won the full confidence of the locals. Then their prisoner of war status changed to free people. Now they could stay there or go almost wherever they wanted. They knew that they were unwanted in Romania and were persecuted, if they returned. Despite all, a few made their way to Germany in the hope of returning from there to their families in the Banat.

My father decided to stay in England for the time being. In his letters he assured us that he wanted to help us as far as was possible. He also wanted to try every possible step, to get us out to the West. Oma had no desire to immigrate. She saw our lives as a known evil and did not want to exchange it for an unknown evil. Because there were in fact no concrete options to leave the country, we were spared from making a decision.

We boys spent many school-free days on the meadow located on both sides of the railway track, where it makes a detour around the village. Sometimes we were looking for cartridges and other spent or live ammunition, primarily along the ditch next to the rails, where the Soviet soldiers had dug in during the battle for the village. We found all kinds of war material, some of which could be dangerous if handled improperly. We learned to distinguish between German and Russian ammunition, and we became progressively bolder in what we collected. One day we found a German hand granate that seemed intact and in good condition. We took it to a Romanian farmer who was working nearby, and asked him to throw it in the fire he had been feeding with weeds. After he finished his work, he threw the hand granate into the fire. We all run about a hundred yards and threw ourselves on the ground. After waiting for what seemed an eternity, we got up and started walking towards the village. Suddenly we heard a big explosion; our hand granate had finally exploded and could no longer hurt anybody.

Another day we walked through some fields situated to the west of the village, which had once been vineyards. Suddenly we came across a half-decayed human body. Part of the red hair was still visible, as was some clothing that we could not identify as civilian or military. There were no shoes and parts of the body were missing, possibly eaten by wild animals. We ran away and did not dare to notify anybody about our discovery.

Perhaps the scariest experience was a walk towards Pakatz. As a group of six or seven boys, we walked on the railway tracks in the direction of Lowrin. When we came close to the buildings of Puszta Pakatz, we crossed some fields to reach the Szegediner highway. The idea was to walk back to the village on that road, on which we could not see or hear any vehicles. Looking back, one of us noticed the dishevelled figure of a man running towards us. We started running for our lives, since the intentions of the man following us did not seem to be friendly. After running for what seemed a very long time, I felt that I was getting tired. Glancing back, I noticed that our pursuer had also stopped running. We all got a breather but continued walking as fast as we could, towards the village.

Mercifully, not all days brought that kind of excitement. On some other days, all the excitement was sitting under the little railway bridge when the train rolled over it.

# 13. Village life goes on

On the way to church, by Hans Roch

Not all farmers in the village had lost their land through expropriation. There was now a new kind of farmers in the village: the so-called "five-hectare" farmers. Most of them were Romanian colonists, our new co-inhabitants. There were also some Germans who had served during World War II only in the Romanian army. They were entitled to possess and cultivate five hectares, or nine "Joche" of land, allocated to them from the large mass of land expropriated from the German farmers. Farmer

Roth was one of the new "five-hectare" farmers. Before the war he had owned many more hectares, but five hectares was better than nothing, and he found that he could actually make a living from that land. Roth had been released from his Romanian unit soon after the end of the war, and came straight home. He was shocked to learn that his wife had been deported to Russia and that his two children had been left alone with their grandmother.

Compared to the majority of the dispossessed farmers, the five-hectare farmers did quite well at the beginning. There was, however, a catch: The state demanded from them a share of the crop, the so-called quota. Over the years, this quota was increased regularly, regardless of the weather-dependent crops. There were years in which some five-hectare farmers had to buy wheat in order to be able to deliver their quotas to the government, because non-compliance could get them to jail. It became clear only later, that the procedure had been planned with forethought: it made it easier later on for many a farmer, to just give up his land and join the collective farm. Many other farmers were trying desperately to preserve their ownership and the small degree of independence that farmers derived from working on their own land.

In the village you could not learn much about it, but there were rumours that mechanic Roos had received an extended prison sentence for his hasty court-martial and the sentencing of his Romanian helper. Farmer Mayer was also supposed to have received a longer prison sentence for his hasty burial of the dead Soviet soldiers. The problem of a permanent burial ground for all the Soviet soldiers killed in the village and its neighbourhood was still far from being solved. At some point, a large grave was dug in the little park surrounding the war memorial. All known casualties of the Red Army were then exhumed from their graves and reburied in that large grave. But this was not meant to be their final resting place. They were again exhumed and reburied in a very large grave topped with a large monument in Großsanktnikolaus. The villagers were shaking their heads and said that these soldiers will not get their bones together on Judgement day. It was obvious that the Soviet dead were treated decently, in contrast with our women, girls and men thrown into the mass graves of Stalino. The Soviets had won the war and we were among the losers of the war. For us, there were once again only tears left.

Little by little we learned the Romanian language in school and on the street. After class, principal Alexandru retained some of us in his room to work on our vocabulary. He always wrote about two dozen words on a blackboard and explained in detail the meaning of each word. We wrote the words in our copybooks, and added our own German translation, as dictionaries were not available. To pay for these private lessons, Oma sewed many clothes for the family of the principal. When a school year was over, a small closing ceremony always took place. As a prize, I received several Romanian books. During the summer holidays I always found the time to read these books, in addition to various German books, from school books to Karl May. At home and in our everyday life, we continued to use our Schwowische dialect. In school we spoke Romanian with the Romanian teachers, and standard German with the German teachers, whatever their language of instruction was at a given moment. With our priest Molnar everybody spoke standard German, as we had learned from our parents and grandparents. Newly added was Romanian. All of it was simply part of our education and it seemed only natural that educated persons had to know the official language of the country, in addition to their native language.

Later on, German classes were slowly reintroduced in our school. Our German teachers had been teaching in the Romanian language at the beginning, as long as the authorities had prescribed it to them. Now they taught German classes in late afternoon, for students who enrolled voluntarily. To nobody's surprise, all German children had enrolled, some because they wanted to learn their native language, others because their parents or grandparents had registered them.

Kerosene lamps were fastened to the ceiling of the classroom and our teacher welcomed us in German. Since German school books were not available, we practiced reading with recent copies of the newspaper "Temeswarer Zeitung". One evening each of us students was asked to write an essay and the teacher collected these papers. To my surprise, I later learned that my paper had been passed around the teachers' office. The teachers were surprised that my essay was essentially free of errors and were wondering "how the guy managed to do that." The explanation was in fact very simple: At home I had always been reading German newspapers, magazines and books, and learned the proper spelling without any conscious effort.

Five years after their deportation, the surviving deportees returned from the Soviet Union. They had been through much, but they had survived. Some of their children could not recognize them and they had to slowly get used to each other. But they had returned home safely and their families were whole again. My mother unfortunately was not there and those returning home only confirmed what we already knew. To our surprise, young neighbour Maria was not among the survivors. Old Maria and Oma often wept together, but stopped crying when we children approached them. One of the returnees brought us a few of my mother's belongings. Among those was a letter in pencil that my mother had written on 27 January 1945, while in a railroad car that they all knew was on its way to the Soviet Union. In this letter, mother writes:

"... Dear child and beloved mother, stay healthy and strong as I want to stay. I want to urge you to persevere. Watch out for your health, we want to be together again some day ...."

Most returnees recovered gradually and were able to occupy their places in the lives of their families. Others never recovered; they were marked by death. Everyone in our neighbourhood knew that a girl from our neighbourhood had become involved with the radio operators. This was a new kind of fraternization, and it was sharply condemned by many village people. When I asked Oma for her views on the subject, she said: "She wants to get some enjoyment out of her life, just like every other human being. And if there are no young German men in the village, she has to make do with what is there". The girl died the following year, at the age of 23 years.

When our priest Molnar was no longer allowed to teach his lessons of religion in the classrooms of the school, he simply moved them to the church or to the parish house. Some of the traditional religious customs were also allowed to continue. Throughout the month of May, evening prayers were held at the church. There was a festive and happy atmosphere, with much song and organ music. At the end of the service, all children gathered in front of the altar, where father Molnar conducted them in a chorus of praise to Jesus. When the voices of the children rose in the twilight of the church, amidst the fragrance of the many spring flowers covering the altars, it was a memorable experience that left nobody untouched.

On All Saints Day, a large procession with banners, song, and music went from the church to a cemetery. In the evening, the villagers went back to the cemetery and lit a multitude of candles on the graves of their relatives. Nobody ever placed food on any of our graves, but the sea of lit candles was a much-revered tradition, and it created a sight to behold. The trip home from the cemetery took place in complete darkness, lit up only by a candle in a lantern, carried by an adult in each family. The evening left behind an unforgettable memory in the minds of young children, many of whom had never been out so late in the evening.

An event as much anticipated as Christmas itself was midnight mass on the night before Christmas Day. It was another occasion for staying up late, for walking through the unlit streets, with the help of only an electric flashlight. I remember making sure that somebody brought back from Temeswar one of those hard-to-get and expensive flashlight batteries and saving it for the walk to midnight mass. The church was again beautifully decorated, with more lit candles than on any other day. Sometimes the organ and church choir were reinforced by an orchestra; sometimes the brass band played in front of the church at the end of the mass. In this exalted mood, even the walk home was beautiful, especially when the snow fell lightly through the trees, making a wonderful sound before reaching the ground.

One spring day in 1946 our priest Molnar did not show up in church for the morning mass. One of the altar boys climbed the wall and unlocked the gate. From the corridor, one could see the priest lying on his bed, but he did not answer to any calls. A doctor was called from somewhere and confirmed that our priest had died of a massive heart attack.

The funeral took place in his native Perjamosch and the whole village of Alexanderhausen was there to accompany our priest on his last trip. People came on bicycles, in horse carriages, and even on foot. Our brass band played its March of the Dead, and the full church choir sang some of its saddest and most beautiful songs. I had never before seen such a united effort by the whole village, and I would never see it again.

# 14. FORBIDDEN SOURCES OF NEWS AND MUSIC

Richard had salvaged a radio of the Telefunken brand from the war, but some of its tubes were missing. One morning we decided to take the unit to Temeswar for repair. The morning train was crowded as always and we both sat on the solid box, during the whole journey from our village to Temeswar. On a street not far from the railway station, we found a small shop whose owner promised to fix the radio, for a price acceptable to Richard. We had already found the necessary flashlight batteries, and the old lead-acid battery was restored after Uncle Gerhard had connected it for a considerable length of time to the electric supply of his corn mill.

Now our own radio stood in Richard's improvised room, a luxury that very few villagers could enjoy in those days. We listened mostly to broadcasting stations from Austria and West Germany. We were surprised that, while the Romanian-language broadcast stations from the West were jammed, the German stations came through loud and clear. Either there were just too many of them, or those responsible for jamming did not care about us Romania-Germans. In this way we maintained a close connection with the West, with the Europe from which we were separated in an arbitrary and unnatural way.

The German songs, the operas and operettas presented in German seemed to us music from a different and forbidden world, from which our leader had arbitrarily excluded us. Even the advertisements sounded good in our ears, because they showed us once again that the West was not society with structural shortages, and that all consumer goods were readily available there. We had to deal every day with these shortages, and we wondered why our workers could not produce, and our stores did not sell the goods demanded by the population.

We were curious about everything that was not available to us. We would have wanted at least a short trip to that Western consumer's paradise.

We wanted to see the articles, even if we did not have the money to buy them. These were certainly very human feelings, but our leaders did not or could not understand them. Instead of taking note of these feelings, we were sprinkled daily with the theories of the superiority of the socialist system. The West was always painted only in black: strikers in France, the homeless in New York, rubble women in the western part of Germany. The propaganda was disseminated through all available media, especially through the press and radio. The political activists had the thankless task of convincing the young and old people of their view of things. Often they achieved just the opposite of the attitude they wanted to change. The majority of people were slowly being convinced that everything was better in the West.

On a hot summer evening we kept the door of Richard's room open and we went out into the yard. On the radio, Chancellor Adenauer was just giving a speech. For some reason, the volume increased suddenly so that the voice of the old Chancellor echoed loudly through the street. We ran back into the room, locked the door and reduced the volume. Thankfully, nobody reported to the authorities that we were listening to a forbidden Western radio station.

It was common knowledge that in our village and other villages in the area, young people had been jailed because they had been singing forbidden songs. Everyone knew that the songs of the Hitler era were forbidden, but the authorities could define at their discretion which Western pop songs were forbidden. Even some old German popular songs or marching songs could be considered bourgeois or reactionary.

Richard and I had listened to the final match of the FIFA World Cup 1954 between Germany and Hungary. We were delighted with the unexpected final result and walked out onto Main Street. The village brass band had been playing somewhere and stopped afterwards at the tavern called "restaurant". There some sports enthusiast described to them the game in glowing colors. As they made their way home, the first horn player stopped in the middle of the main street and produced the first bars of the German national anthem. The second horn player had already reached the next street corner, two hundred meters down the main street. From there he responded with the succeeding bars of the well-known song. Many villagers heard this duo with surprise and perhaps even sang along. They did not know or care what verse was allowed or used in the West.

# 15. VILLAGE LIFE AND SCHOOL REFORMS

Our daily bread, by Hans Roch

At some point the government and the communist party had to give some thought to the economic situation in the country. They decided that everyone regardless of their language and culture should contribute to the building of socialism. Maybe they remembered something of the socialist principles established by Marx and Engels. A German department was established in the village schools and German folk dances were also performed again. Even the previously forbidden Kirchweih was allowed to be celebrated, albeit with a socialist rather than a religious flavour. The dispossessed farmers did not get their fields back, but they could become members of the new collective farms. There they could work together on the pooled fields, almost like Uncle Gerhard had described it years ago in pastel colors.

But Uncle Gerhard could not be found among the brigades of field workers. His land had been confiscated; his shredder, tractor and threshing machine had been expropriated and were now state property. He still wanted to do something for the community, so he found somewhere an electric generator, connected it to his old but still usable diesel engine and thus established the first electric power station in the village. From the day it started operations, it lit up the village streets in the evenings. Many welcomed this progress, others hated it. Gradually, more and more homes were connected to the small community network.

Since no electricity meters were available, people paid for the number of installed lamps or electrical appliances. Inevitably, some people concluded that if they have to pay for each light bulb, then they may as well keep it lit all night. As a result, the generator was often overloaded and switched off automatically for its self-protection. Uncle Gerhard requested a larger generator, but none could be found. Despite his objections, more houses were connected to the electricity supply. The generator now turned itself off regularly, night after night, and the old familiar darkness spread throughout the village. After the generator cooled down, Uncle Gerhard returned it to service, but the overload prevented it from providing service for a long time.

The process was obvious to every knowledgeable person, but was not understood by the local authorities, or by the newspaper writers. Perhaps the situation was deliberately presented in a false light, because it provided a wonderful opportunity to expose the class enemy. Soon an article was published in the newspaper, which claimed that Uncle Gerhard had fun every evening, turning off the power and plunging the working people of the community in the dark. This false report upset Uncle Gerhard, because he wanted to be really proud of his contribution to the welfare of the community. But he was powerless against the newspaper report, because in the eyes of the party he was just another of those rich German kulaks, a class enemy. His long-standing sympathies for the Soviet Union and his support of the underground Communist Party of Romania during the war years simply could not change that basic fact.

Soon the first of the former villagers now living in the Federal Republic of Germany returned to the village as visitors. They were the same former SS men who only a few years earlier would have been prosecuted and imprisoned. Now they were welcome as visitors because they brought foreign currency into the country and some could perhaps be persuaded to stay there. One of the first visitors was Adam Gilde, who arrived by train. Then my Schneider Uncle came by railway. Later on, many came with their own cars. They visited their fathers, mothers, siblings and sometimes their wives and children. Only one man decided to stay with his family in the village. Most of the visitors analyzed with their families the means that could be used to enable and accelerate the migration of other family members. When the first children were allowed to join their parents abroad, the villagers took note that emigration was not totally impossible. As a result, many villagers found new hope that they would escape from their misery. For many, years or decades had to pass before this hope was fulfilled. For others, this hope has never been fulfilled.

The village kept on changing. The inn, with its large ballroom had become the so-called home of culture. For a time, there was a reading club with Romanian and German newspapers and magazines. It was more difficult with the radio, because they did not want to allow the villagers to find western radio stations. The solution imposed from above was to keep the radio locked up in a separate room, with only the loudspeakers in the club rooms open to the public.

The former small farmer Buchner had also acquired socialist or Marxist ideas, just like Uncle Gerhard. In contrast to Gerhard, he was not rich, so he could now become a party member. He was assigned to do educational work among German youth. When a group of us stood outside the restaurant, Buchner joined us and joined in on our conversation. He asked how we liked the new life in the village and whether we could think of any improvements. He explained that such improvements were certainly possible if we only became members of the communist youth organization UTM. He told us that he wanted to see a German majority in that organization. When nobody answered, he said that we should carefully consider our views and then went away. Some of us were wondering what his superiors in the party would have thought of this nationalist approach to communist youth work.

Almost every Saturday night, there was now dancing in the "home of culture", attended by the more mature youth but not by us, the youngsters.

One Saturday evening our school organized a school celebration on the stage of the "home of culture", followed by dancing to the music of the Tschora Hans orchestra. The name of the orchestra leader was actually Hans Frauenhoffer and he and his group came from the village of Ostern. When the school celebration was over, we were allowed to stay for a while and listen to the music. Tschora Hans showed his talent as a singer and accordionist. The applause seemed endless, and he had to repeat the song "Mariandl-andl-andl" several times. During the following days, some boys at school claimed to know that during a long break, Hans had disappeared from the dance hall with a young woman whose husband had remained in the West. In those days of torn-apart families, this event did no longer result in the woman being ostracized. The times had certainly changed.

The two men from our village who had gone to England with my father had settled in well. Being free people they could go or stay wherever they wanted. My father decided to immigrate to Canada, which seemed to him a country of the future, not least also for me, if he could find a way of getting me there. It did not take long for the young Cherier to marry his English girlfriend. The older Franz Dinjer lived with the woman, whose fields he had taken over. One day his left-behind wife visited us in a state of great disturbance. She spoke very loudly and was crying between her words. She asked Oma to write to my father and ask him to appeal to her husband's conscience and ask him to think about the wife and children he had left behind here at home. Oma promised to do so in her next letter, but added that it was certainly impossible for Mr. Dinjer to forget his own family. As for entering into a second marriage, he had to answer only to his conscience. It was rumoured in the village that the woman in England was expecting a child. Whether that was true or not, could not be verified under the given circumstances.

One of the many education reforms eliminated the junior cycle of high school. When we reached the seventh grade, the question of what to do next became acute for us and for our parents or guardians. Oma asked director Alexandru for his advice. He convinced her that there was only one way forward for me. I should first attend high school in Temeswar, to be followed by university studies. Oma mentioned our limited resources, but the principal would have none of it. He claimed there was not the slightest doubt that I would receive a scholarship in the secondary school of my choice. Furthermore, he was sure that after finishing secondary school, I would receive a scholarship for university. In his opinion, the most assured path for progressing through high school and university would be through a Romanian-language high school.

At that time my father was still in England and sent us his approval in a letter from there. He mentioned at the same time that, unfortunately, he could not help us as much as he would like. Sending money was out of the question, because the possession of foreign currency was forbidden by law, and any remittances of foreign currency were not handed over, but exchanged in Lei only at the official exchange rate. It was common knowledge that the official exchange rate at that time was only about a tenth of the actual purchase value of Western currencies. That was a form of exploitation to which we could not subject my father. Oma and I were well on our own for cash

My father had previously sent us a parcel about every other month. Oma had to pick those up in Temeswar, after paying the customs charges. These customs charges rose to exceed the trading price of the sent objects. We had to ask my father to send only the occasional parcels, with items that were either not available in Romania, or could be sold for a profit.

Clothing received from the West could also trigger unexpected events. A friend had received very tight blue jeans from a relative in the West. At the time, these jeans were banned in Romania. When he walked down the Corso promenade in Temeswar wearing these tight jeans, he was arrested by the militia as "Malagambist", a term applied to people imitating so-called decadent Western habits. I had to ask my father not to send me this type of garments. The parcels from my father became less frequent, but continued sporadically even after his emigration from England to Canada. In time I became the proud owner of several suits and a Timex watch.

At our graduation ceremony, principal Alexandru made a memorable speech in which he congratulated us graduates to our success and wished us the best for the future. With visible emotion, he said that he had never seen a class like ours, and he was sure that he would never see one again. We had begun the third grade with the Romanian primer, since none of us German children spoke any Romanian. Now we all spoke fluent Romanian, and knew the written language as well as our Romanian classmates. After a common meal in one of the classrooms, a dance party came about, and I played the violin in the improvised orchestra. It was the first time that I did that, but it was also the last time, because later on I never had time for violin lessons.

The closing ceremony had an interesting sequel. It came from one of our teachers, the one with a moustache, generally called catfish by the class. He came from Bessarabia or Bukovina, and it was common knowledge that he was actually a lawyer by profession. In his class, he had the thankless task of getting us acquainted with the Constitution of the Romanian People's Republic. Now he asked those of us who were preparing for the high school entrance examination to join him in a classroom. He wanted to give us some clues about the art of successfully passing those tests. He stressed that what we needed to supply was not our personal opinion, or even the truth, but solely the politically correct answer. He explained this game of question and answer with some examples that were very daring for that time. We admired his extraordinary openness and courage, and thanked him sincerely. Later I had to think of him often, because I had numerous opportunities to apply the advice received from him.

# 16. Commuting between village and city

Soon after our graduation ceremony we had to face the entrance examination for high school in Temeswar. The morning train arrived in Temeswar shortly after six o'clock. Richard and I had all the time for walking to the Domplatz, or Cathedral Square. It turned out that there were still some forms to be filled out in the office, before we were admitted to the large examination hall. The candidates had already taken their seats, but Richard and I found two empty seats. I looked at our fellow candidates and was surprised that they all seemed to be older, more mature, or somehow more sophisticated than us village boys. For a moment, my only thought was: What are we village boys doing here among all these clever city boys? Did we really have a chance of being admitted to this high school?

We completed the tests the same day and took the evening train back to the village. The truth is that I was pretty sure that I had done well. The results were supposed to be posted two weeks later on the bulletin board of the high school. I avoided the trip to Temeswar because it cost money. For several weeks, we did not know the results of the entrance examination. Later that summer, Richard took the train to Temeswar and brought back the good news. He was excited when he said: "We have been admitted. As expected, your name is at the top of the list". I had learned an important lesson for the future: Even in Temeswar, the soup was still made with water. Richard was right when he said: "What they know, we know too, and you are likely to know more than that."

After much deliberation, Richard and I decided to start high school as commuters. We would take the morning train to the city and return to the village with the evening train. It was not only the most economical alternative, but it also had the advantage that I could continue to stay in the familiar village with Oma, maintaining what was left of my family for a few more years.

The classes began on a Monday in September and it was still dark when I arrived at the village railway station. To my surprise, Richard appeared with his grandfather, who was pushing a bicycle fully laden with bedding beside him. I pretended that I did not notice the two, but I knew instantly that they had found lodging for Richard in Temeswar, where his grandmother had several relatives. Richard later came back to the village every Saturday and we could continue to exchange our experiences. When spring arrived, Richard joined me as a commuter.

Life as commuters had its good and its bad sides. The worst was getting up very early every day except Sunday, so that I could be at the railway station at five thirty in the morning. Since we had no alarm clock, I had to completely rely on our very reliable wall clock. There was no electricity in the village, either Oma or I had to get up and light a match to check the time. A better method was needed, so I took out the little electric bulb from my flashlight and installed it next to the dial of the clock. Then I run a pair of wires to a flashlight battery and a small switch next to my bed. Now I could check the time by just pushing the button. But most of the time it was still Oma who woke me up on time. As it was very early in the morning and I was always in a hurry, a real breakfast was out of the question. Sometimes I quickly drank a cup of tea, while Oma put a sandwich in my pocket, maybe an apple or a handful of plums, if they were available. That had to be sufficient until dinner.

On most days, the morning train was crowded. There were workers, students, market women and villagers from the surrounding villages, from Grosssanktnikolaus to Neubeschenowa, who had something to do in the city. The workers and students wanted nothing more than the cabin lights switched off, so that they could sleep. The market women wanted nothing more than to keep talking, with their voices at maximum loudness. Sometimes one of the workers or students let out a long "Sssssss" sound, the hiss of the geese, and the women stopped talking. After a short time, the chatter continued. One morning, a worker gave each of us a piece of newspaper and some dry tobacco leaves. We made cigarettes and lit them all at the same time. The compartment quickly filled with a raspy smoke. The women fled from the compartment as fast as they could. We opened a couple of windows to vent and then continued to sleep undisturbed.

One autumn morning, some women from our village boarded the train with sacks that seemed destined for the market. The following morning there were more women and some men with sacks. In the sacks they had carrots, collected in the fields of the state agricultural enterprise, after the regular harvest was over. But no secret could be kept in the community, and so the next morning, the militiamen appeared at the station. They confiscated all the bags and took the owners of the bags to their militia station. The people had lost their carrots and had nothing to show for their work, but they escaped with a warning and a lecture about the sanctity of state property.

The process reminded me of a case that had occurred several years earlier. In the meadow towards Neusiedel there were three large straw piles. They were left over from the summer of 1945, when threshing of the wheat acquired from the expropriated Germans took place on that meadow. The piles were still there the following year, as the state enterprise simply could not find any use for the straw. Many villagers could use the straw only too well and helped themselves to small quantities of it. The leaders of the State Agricultural Enterprise found a way out of this unacceptable situation: the straw piles were simply set on fire and burned to ashes in front of the villagers. Uncle Gerhard shook his head and said: "In our workers' and peasants' state, all goods are supposed to belong to the workers, but as property of the state they are untouchable." He might have added: "And the party alone determines what happens to all state property, even if it is just leftover carrots or excess straw."

In front of the Central Railway Station appeared a rather large caricature. A portly man in a fancy uniform carried a huge axe, from which the blood was dripping. Underneath there was an inscription in large letters: "Down with Tito the traitor, who sold out his people." We had heard about his butchering of Serbia's ethnic Germans, and thought that the "butcher" epithet was appropriate. But now he had apparently upset the "great Stalin" to get that kind of treatment. On another day, a few years later, the Central Station was suddenly closed down to all civilians, with soldiers posted all around it. When the Station reopened in the afternoon, word spread rapidly, that Tito had arrived by special train, for a meeting with Romanian or Soviet high party officials. The assumption that fences were being mended was confirmed by newspaper articles appearing in the following days. Tito had again become "persona grata", a communist and an ally.

In the spring, Richard's grandparents somehow procured a children's bike for him. One Sunday he lent it to me and I learned to ride a bicycle. Later on Richard progressed to an adult bike. Once again, his grandparents had bought the bike from mysterious vendors in Temeswar. Since we were almost adults now, the transition to a full size bike was pretty easy. Of a motorcycle or a car we could only dream and so the bicycles became our principal means of locomotion.

For me, all that was available was my father's bicycle that I had rescued from the expropriation commission. To make it operational, we disassembled it first into its component parts and cleaned each one with kerosene. Then we put them all back together and oiled the various parts. Now I was the happy owner of a vehicle. Unfortunately I had to register it at the village hall and that cost money. Grandma earned some money from her work with the sewing machine and gave me the necessary sum without me having to ask for it.

Richard and I started with small trips to Neusiedel, Billed and Bogarosch. In the summer we frequently went to the beach on the Marosch. On the gravel-covered Szegediner highway we drove in the direction of Lowrin, to a country road that branched off from the highway in the direction of Pesak. From there, a well-travelled footpath next to the road led to Perjamosch. On the footpath our bikes rolled really well. Oma's experience with bathing in the Marosch had instilled in me a good measure of respect for this river. It was the greatest river I had ever seen and the eddy currents in its centre were often visible. In the village pond called Sandkaul, many of us boys had learned to swim on our backs. In the village there were no swimming lessons; the facilities were missing, resulting in a lack of both opportunity and interest.

From our bathing trips to the Marosch during the summer, we always were very thirsty when we came back to Pesak. We usually parked our bikes in front of the village inn, officially called "the restaurant". We were willing to give a kingdom for a beer. Unfortunately, beer was often not available and we had to share a pint of wine and mineral water. We kept asking ourselves why our breweries could not produce enough beer, while the breweries in the West apparently had no such problems.

Once we went to Triebswetter on our bikes, to buy wine. After we tasted the wine in several houses, our bikes seemed to run by themselves. We were a little tipsy, but we reached home without any problems. For the longer distance to Temeswar we used a different approach. One of us drove the bicycle to Temeswar and returned to Alexanderhausen by train, while the other took the train to Temeswar and came back on the bike.

Our longest trip by far was to Nadrag, where Richard's aunt lived. On the first day of this trip, we drove to Lugosch via Temeswar. It was evening when we reached Lugosch, and since we had no lights on our bikes, we had to get off the bikes and push them through the centre of the city. That was the law and we wanted to avoid any conflict with it. In the centre of the city we found a hotel room, placed the bicycles in the middle of the room and fell into our beds in total exhaustion.

In the morning we awoke to the sound of martial music, because it was the 23$^{rd}$ of August, the day on which the liberation of the country by the Red Army was celebrated. The air around us reeked to the heavens, and a terrible smell of decay filled the room. We followed our noses and traced the smell to a bag attached to Richard's bike. In it, his grandmother had packed two chickens. The chickens were ready to roast, but raw. Richard's grandmother had meant well, but the warm August day had caused the chicken to rot. We did not simply leave the package at the hotel, because the prospect of having to explain the origin of the smell was not very tempting. We took the smelly bag with us until after several kilometres we reached a hill of impressive height. There we stopped and Richard threw the chicken into a ravine, while wishing the wild animals living there a good appetite.

Around noon, we reached our destination, the terminus of a narrow-gauge railway, on which we counted to get us to Nadrag. Everything went according to plan and soon our bikes were standing in the middle of an open car of the narrow gauge railway. We sat next to them and admired the increasingly hilly landscape that was so new to us. When we arrived in Nadrag, the celebration of National Liberation Day was in full swing. A man carrying a large piece of wood was running after another man. Did he want to kill him or just beat him up? We concluded that the working class was indeed revolutionary in this working class settlement, especially on a holiday with high alcohol consumption. It must be admitted that the rough manners in this Wild West of the Banat hills scared us just a little bit.

Richard's aunt was very happy to see us, even though we had arrived without the chicken. During the next few days we hiked through the mountains and admired each and every gorge and waterfall, because we had never seen anything like them in the lowlands around Alexanderhausen. The planned ascent to the summit of the Padesch peak could not be completed because of continues bad weather at higher altitudes.

The days passed quickly and soon we were again sitting on the narrow gauge railway car. When we reached Rekasch later in the day, it started to rain. We had no raincoats and soon were wet through and through. As we were moving along a footpath beside the road, suddenly a cow was standing in front of my bike, blocking the footpath. I drove closer to the cow, but she did not budge. When I stopped and tried to push the bike around her, the beast stepped right in the middle of the spokes of my front wheel. We stopped, removed the front wheel of my bike, let out the air and straightened out the wheel by hammering it with a rock as much as we could. We got the bike back on the road, with the front wheel looking a little like a figure eight. By the time we reached Temeswar, our clothes were dry again. We spent the night in Temeswar, and reached Alexanderhausen the following day in time for lunch, exhausted but satisfied with our performance.

Now we needed a good rest before school started again. We sat in the grass in our garden and talked about the successful trip to the mountains. We also remembered that Richard's aunt had complained about her small pension and mentioned her desire to leave for Germany if it ever became possible.

In spring and autumn, life as a commuter was at its best. On the train, the windows were usually open, fresh air from the fields filled the compartment and we enjoyed life. The boys and girls from the village of Billed usually sat together and someone broke into a song. Sometimes they sang old German folk songs, sometimes the last hit from the West. When I close my eyes I can still hear a song: ". . . Just ask your heart, if loyalty it can break . . ." We had heard the song a few times on Richard's radio, but were surprised that the Billeder knew the full text. Some of them must have listened to the forbidden radio stations of the West, or some relative had sent them the notes and lyrics from the West?

Some former classmates and I had made friends with three girls from Neubeschenowa. They attended a trade school located near the "Maria Monument". Their school uniform consisted of fairly short black dresses with white collars. Some mornings we accompanied them from the Central Railway Station to their school. We walked behind them and exchanged comments that were meant to be funny and sometimes even were funny. My former classmates claimed to have noticed that the pretty brunette often smiled at me. They designated her as my girlfriend. I did not mind it, but I knew that our plans of going out with the girls would remain only dreams. In Temeswar, we had no time to even invite the girls to see a movie. Their village was too far away from Alexanderhausen to consider weekend visits. We had to accept that on the weekend our girls took part in the only entertainment available in the village, the dances in the cultural centre of their village. And we could not take part in that entertainment.

At the Temeswar Central Station, I often spent part of the afternoon with two classmates from a Banat village famous for its wine, waiting for our evening trains. We noticed three girls who were also waiting every day for the departure of their train. It was not hard to determine that their destination was the village of Sackelhausen. There were many afternoons, when we were all sitting or standing in the large waiting room, with us looking at them, and them looking at us. We wanted to talk to the girls and it seemed that the girls wanted to talk to us. Why else would the blonde girl with the blue eyes look at us that way? But how could we talk to the girls without being formally introduced? We could not simply walk over and introduce ourselves. We concluded that we had to ask the girls if they were interested in talking with us. We decided to ask the question in writing. I formulated the big question on a piece of paper and one of my friends took it over to the girls. They seemed to discuss the issue, but we had to go on to our respective trains before we received an answer.

We continued to sit in two separate groups and exchanged just looks and sometimes a wink or a smile. I had almost forgotten about the story, when many years I learned that one of my two colleagues had actually married the blonde girl with the blue eyes. But before that, he had to complete high school and study medicine for six full years.

Once again I spent the summer at home in Alexanderhausen. I had managed to borrow a considerable number of books, because the holidays were often reading time. The books were a mixed bag, from Karl May to Karl Marx. One evening after a hot summer day I took a walk through the village. There was no moon and no street lighting and the streets were enveloped in total darkness. I stopped at the communal well in the Rondell which had the indisputably best drinking water in the village. I pulled down the lever at the pump a few times and drank the cool water. Suddenly Gretchen stood before me and she was obviously thirsty. She was a pretty girl, a few years younger than me, and we had run into each other at school a few times. We talked about this and that, as we walked slowly in the direction of her home. I was amazed how open and reasonable she was and how you could talk to her about any subject. She had recently started to attend the Saturday night dances in the cultural centre, with her girlfriends. She asked me if I would come to those dances, and it sounded in my ears like a very promising suggestion. Or was it like a siren song? I muttered something about lack of time and added that if I attended, it would only be with her. To my great surprise, she said that would be really nice.

We had arrived outside her house and she gave me a goodbye kiss. Now I knew why the well was known in the village as the "kissing well". On my way home I tried to review my perceptions about my present and my future. My ultimate goal, even though it was still wrapped in dense fog, was emigration. I had no doubt that as a single person I had a better chance to reach that goal, than with a family. Therefore I needed to avoid anything that could lead to marriage and family. I did not want to seduce a girl and then leave her; there was already way too much misery in the world, and I was not going to add to it. I could only imagine a great love to be permanent, not subject to the constraints imposed by a totalitarian government. For the sake of the future, I needed to stay single and unattached.

It was understandable that for the girls of the village, the Saturday-evening dances at the cultural centre were the centre of their lives, around which everything else revolved. For a boy, not to participate was something like social suicide. But participation cost time and money. Realistically, I had little free time and even less money. But even more important was the fact that, by participating, I would increase the danger of drifting into those entanglements that I had to avoid at all costs.

My conclusion once again was that I had to stay alone and independent in order to maximize my chances for emigration. It was necessary to avoid all occasions that could lead to involvement. I knew very well that such a renunciation would not be an easy task, but when was I ever afraid of taking on a tough job? Did our fathers not have to take on much more difficult tasks? Would I not feel like a weakling, if I was not able to accept the necessary sacrifices?

In the following days I repeated this thought several times and always came back to the same conclusion: I had to maintain optimal chances for emigration, and that meant that I had to stay single and independent. I decided to make this fact the cornerstone of my life for the years to come, and named this self-imposed obligation my imperative.

# 17. ANOTHER DEPORTATION

In the spring, on some sunny Sunday afternoons, a few boys of my age group met for a stroll through the village. We discussed the events and experiences of the week, and sometimes watched a game of handball or football, if one was being played on the sports field. I remember well that we did that on a Sunday of 1951. We walked down the main street and then followed the paved walkway toward the sports ground and train station. The sports field was empty, meaning that no game was being played, so we walked to the train station. There we were surprised by a row of cattle cars standing on one of the three railway tracks. We all knew that at this time of year there was nothing to export, no grains, no potatoes, not even pigs. The presence of the cattle cars was therefore a mystery to us.

The next day I had an exam in Temeswar. As always in these days of commuting, I got up at five o'clock in the morning and made my way to the station. The morning light was not quite able to overcome the darkness when I approached the sports field. Suddenly, a uniformed figure stood before me and yelled in Romanian: "Stop! Where are you going?"

A few steps behind the first soldier I could make out a second soldier spread out behind a machine gun. I explained that I was a commuter and was taking the train to Temeswar, where I had a test at my high school. I took out my monthly commuter pass from my pocket and handed it to the soldier. After some hesitation he handed back the commuter pass and indicated that I could proceed. I went to the station, with the queasy feeling in my stomach that my life was now in the hands of the soldier with machine gun.

The train was nearly empty; I had never seen it as empty before. During the test, my thoughts kept returning to the events in our village. The military had to have something to do with the cattle cars, but I could not imagine what it could be. I returned to the village in another nearly empty train in the evening, and found the railway station totally overcrowded. Some militiamen and soldiers pushed me directly to the exit toward the main street. This was not my usual way home, but I was relieved to leave the station behind me. I hurried home as fast as I could. I found Oma in the house and the horror in her face as she told me what had been happening in the village during the day.

That morning some villagers woke up to find a soldier in front of their house. The soldier told them that they had to leave their house immediately, but were allowed to take some belongings and even some animals with them. The soldier was responsible to accompany them and their belongings to the railway station. The panic was great, because once again no one knew the destination of the people being deported. Some were afraid that they were being taken to the Soviet Union, as it had happened in the winter of 1945. Not until the train was well under way was it announced that their destination this time was closer to home. It was the Bărăgan steppe, an inhospitable area located somewhere behind Bucharest and close to the river Danube. They were being removed from the border zone next to Yugoslavia because they were considered unreliable elements. Since any correspondence with the people left behind was forbidden, it took a long time before we found out that they had to survive the first winter in burrows that they had to dig themselves.

But who had placed their names on the list of unreliables? Was the list made by one person, such as Buchner? Were other people involved in making the list? What were the criteria for producing the list? Once again there were no answers to these questions. Some people believed that Buchner or other persons or authorities had placed on the list people such as their enemies, or other villagers whom they did not like or with whom they had a quarrel.

This second deportation produced a few empty houses and quite a few colonists could now move into larger or better maintained houses. Among the deportees were not only German families, but also Romanian ones, especially those that had come from Bessarabia and Bukovina. Many of the remaining Bessarabians and Bukovinians left the village and went into hiding in other areas of Romania. To their neighbours in the village they just indicated that they were returning "to Bucharest".

Many families suffered greatly from the absence of their loved ones. In addition, no one knew whether the authorities had plans for further deportations. There were rumours that all Germans would be expelled from the Banat and resettled elsewhere in the country. Even people who had not previously thought about emigration now came to the conclusion that there was no future for them and their children in the Banat. Many were now convinced that their countrymen who had run away to the West had chosen the better alternative. One could only envy them for it and hope to join them somewhere in the West, whether it was in Germany or Austria, or anywhere else in the free world.

When the party and government decided to complete the collectivization of agriculture in our village, they did not count on farmer Reiter. He had worked hard on his five hectares of land and had done his best to live in good agreement with the authorities. He had always delivered his quota of wheat on time and performed any other obligations that came his way. He wanted to live more like his Swabian ancestors, taking pride in his property and in the results of his own work. Several summonses to the town hall and the educational efforts of Buchner could not move him to join the collective farm. He had decided for himself that he would not join the collective farm under any circumstances.

One evening, a black car stopped in front of the house of the Reiter family. Two men invited Reiter for a car ride. They told him that they had important news for him. One of the men tried in a very friendly tone to explain to Reiter the importance of joining the collective. They drove around the village several times, but Reiter insisted that entry into the collective farm was voluntary, as described in all newspapers.

Two days later, the night drive was repeated. Now the second man took part in the conversation and his words were all but friendly, they actually sounded like implied threats. Reiter remained stubborn. They asked him repeatedly to reconsider. During the next drive, they placed an application form and a pencil in front of Reiter and asked him to sign the document. When he was still reluctant, one of the men spoke up: "So far we have shown great patience with you. But now that all farmers in the village have become members of the collective farm, only an enemy of the people could refuse to join." When Reiter did not make a move to sign, the other man turned to the driver and said: "Turn the car around. We are going to Temeswar. There they know how to deal with enemies of the people."

Reiter put his signature on the application for membership and was promptly taken to his home. The next day the newspaper announced a new success of the collectivization: Alexanderhausen was now fully collectivized.

# 18. Politehnica Timișoara

The author, 1956

All things have a beginning and an end, sometimes even an unexpected one. That is exactly what happened at the end of my high school studies. In the middle of the year in which I was in the tenth grade, our high school was instructed by its higher authorities that the country needed more high school graduates. Therefore, the school was to identify students who were willing to write the high school graduation exams right after the completion of the tenth grade. It was an opportunity to save the costs of an entire school year, a relief for both Oma and me. I immediately accepted the nomination and went on to pass the necessary examinations.

The unexpected early graduation from high school and the results achieved provided a boost to my confidence. I decided to study electrical engineering at the Technical University of Temeswar/Timisoara, locally known as "Politehnica" in Romanian and "Polytechnikum" in German. As a child in a village without electricity, I had admired the electric installation of the village mill. Ever since, the mysteries of electricity had always fascinated me. The marks achieved in the high school graduation examinations were good enough for admission to the Polytechnikum without an entrance exam. I enrolled at the Faculty of Electrical Engineering with the confidence that more good work would maintain the indispensable scholarship.

Oma was thrilled with my decision as always and promised me all the support that she would be able to provide. My father was also pleased, but seemed just a little concerned about my assurance that I could carry this five-year course of studies to a successful conclusion. We all knew that materially he could contribute very little. But what was really certain in this country and in these uncertain times? I was ready to spare no effort to reach my new goal. My reply to my father was that without risk, nothing could be accomplished.

Grandma and I also knew that my life as a commuter had now come to an end. My scholarship provided me with a place to stay in a student home and meals in the student cafeteria, meaning that my basic needs were met. It was clear to us that we had to make more sacrifices, but that there was no reasonable alternative. I promised Oma to take good care of myself and to visit back home as often as possible.

In the fall, the home for the first-year students was a confiscated mansion located across the street from the Catholic Church of the district called Josefstadt. In our room there were 14 first-year students. The toilet worked only rarely and the showers never. But my worst problem was caused by the bedbugs. For some unknown reason, they liked me better than all the other students in the room. In response to my complaints, the caretakers of the building spread more and more gray DDT powder, until it covered bed sheets, blankets and pillows. The effort was largely unsuccessful, because the bedbugs jumped down from the ceiling like paratroopers.

Shortly after Christmas we had to face our first exam in university. We had four study days before the exam and I went home to the village. There it was quiet, and I was able to enjoy Oma's cooking. When I returned to the city the night before the exam, I found my room mates in a state of panic. Almost half of my colleagues had not passed the math exam. I had worked through the material only once, but very thoroughly. Now it seemed to me that I should have done more, but it was too late for that. The next day I passed the exam with the highest mark. This experience reinforced my confidence that I could tackle these exams with calm and confidence, provided that I was rested. During the following three semesters, I passed three more examinations in higher mathematics, all with all the same top marks.

When I returned to Temeswar after the winter vacations and was just about to unpack my suitcase, we were informed that we had to evacuate the student home immediately. We were placed temporarily in the reading room of the student dormitory located in a former hotel near the Central Station. To escape the mess, on Saturday night I took the train home to the village. When I came back early on Monday morning, a stranger was sleeping in what had been my bed. When I questioned him, he told me that my colleagues had already moved into their permanent home. It was located in the Inner City, opposite the large food store called "Alimentara". The building had housed a unit of the Red Army. It seemed that the leaders of the Soviet soldiers had decided that they preferred to live in our mansion located in the Josefstadt. It obviously did not bother them that several hundred students had to be relocated in the process. Thus, the Soviet troops moved into our dilapidated mansion in the Josefstadt and we students moved into their ancient building in the Inner City. My main concern during the transition was whether there would be bedbugs in our new student home.

Our new student residence was an ancient building, and the Russians had dismantled everything not firmly nailed down. All light bulbs and even their fixtures were missing. Workers were busy everywhere repairing the damage to make the building habitable. Whoever had made up the room allocations, had obviously forgotten about me, and no unoccupied bed could be found. I spent the following weeks in a dormitory located on Cathedral Square, again in a large hall. The bedbugs here seemed even hungrier than the ones in the old mansion in the Josefstadt.

After I finally moved back into the dormitory with my colleagues, I did not want to miss any further lectures. I knew that according to the law, I was obliged to go to the police and have my new address officially recorded on my identity card. I had not found the time to do so. One morning, two militiamen were standing at the exit of our student residence and proceeded to check the identity cards of the students as they were leaving the building. Almost half the students had not yet made the required change of address. Our identity cards were confiscated, and we had to step aside. Then our group was set up in rows of four in the middle of the street. Under the supervision of the two militia officers, we marched down the street, to the office of the militia. Ordinary people could certainly see that the authorities knew how to deal with a bunch of law-breaking students.

The academic year came to a successful conclusion and I went back home once again, to our village. I had only a few days off, because before the actual holiday I had to complete an internship in the metallurgical enterprise of Reschitza. These were wonderful days in the village, ideally placed between spring and summer. Acacia blossoms and birdsong were everywhere in the air.

Living in the same house with the family of Romanian colonists had become a lot easier. With the husband once again gone "to Bucharest", only the wife and daughter remained in our house. The two women had decided that they only needed the secondary building. They used the summer kitchen and had set up the former workshop of my father as a bedroom. Oma and I effectively used the main building of our house and nobody had to pass through our kitchen.

The daughter had grown up with me and had been treated by my friends and me mostly as one of the boys. She had spent the last couple of years at a school of the textile industry in Temeswar. I had not seen her for a long time and could not believe that she had become a really attractive girl. We chatted for hours in the yard and I could hardly turn my eyes away from her. Oma considered it necessary to warn me that the girl was "not for me".

The day before my departure, we stood next to the hallway wall and chatted as usual. I learned that her mother was staying a few days in the neighbouring village. During the day, I was preoccupied with trying to figure out why she had told me that. Was it just coincidence or could it be more than that? The day passed slowly and it was already dark when I returned from a walk through the village. I walked as quietly as possible through the yard and put my ear to the window of the workshop. One thing I could determine immediately: She was still awake. But was she alone? Every ounce of blood in my body rose to my head. I just had to find out the truth. I pressed the door handle down slowly and quietly, and the door was not locked. In a single ineffable moment I held her in my arms and with a myriad of kisses the world disappeared like in a vast sea of fire. When I woke up again and tried to kiss her, I found only tears: "Little girl, how can you cry when I am so unspeakably happy?"

"I know that you will go away again and leave me here alone. That makes me very sad."

"But you know that I have to finish the school that I began, because without that, there could be no life. The future is hidden from both of us, but I could never forget you."

The next day I took the train via Temeswar to Reschitza, where my colleagues had already arrived. Our small group decided to make the most of the summer, as it was after all the largest part of our summer vacation. We hiked through the surrounding woods and filled our water bottles at the springs in the forest. We passed through the caves and walked through the Semenik mountains. During one of the trips I stumbled over a stone and a colleague walking behind me asked, "Man, where are your thoughts?" I gave him the only true answer. "At home" I said and he understood and did not ask any further questions.

Some days I was suffering from a previously unknown type of homesickness. I said to myself that somewhere out there, real life went on, while I felt uprooted and alone, even in the midst of my colleagues. It seemed to me that I had taken on too heavy a burden with my imperative, because the true, real guidelines could only be set by life itself. On other days, my hard-won and so far respected imperative stood firm. I had accepted it on the basis of logic and after much reflection. It was still the best way to ensure a better future.

When our internship was finished I stepped off the train in Alexanderhausen full of expectation and insecurity. At home, all windows and doors of the secondary building stood open, but no one was visible. As I stood there and looked at the empty building, Oma said: "They moved out during the night and without saying goodbye. No one knows where they went, but they are no longer in the village". My first thought was, most likely "to Bucharest".

I decided not to tell anybody about the fairy tale that had passed so quickly. It would remain my secret, a beautiful dream that was over all too quickly. On one of the following evening I found myself walking through our garden, humming to myself a tune from a well-known operetta:

". . . And all fairy tales start with: Once upon a time . . ." For a moment only, my thoughts went back to the girl that had moved away. I wished her a happy a life, wherever she would spend it. Although no one could hear it, I said out loud a few times: I will not forget you, Viorica.

The fact that the newly created reality was a return to status quo ante sank in rather slowly. But eventually my imperative regained its full weight, and I was more determined than ever. In the remaining weeks of vacation, Richard and I took out our bikes as often as we could. In the evenings we took long walks through the village. After the heat of the day, the evenings were pleasantly warm and perfectly suited for talks about God and the world.

We were lodged in the same student dormitory building for the following academic year, but we received a smaller room accommodating only four students. We had access to a shared study hall, but we had no working showers. Every Friday and Saturday evenings we could use the large communal shower room of the student residence belonging to the Faculty of Mechanical Engineering. In the third year we finally moved into the modern student residence of the Faculty of Mechanical Engineering. We were only three students in a room and we had the working showers downstairs in the same building. Even the cafeteria was next door, so that long walks to the eatery were no longer required. The rooms even had central heating and each one had a functioning sink. The most important thing was that there were no bedbugs.

The sports field of the Polytechnic lay at our feet and from some of the rooms one could watch the matches of handball and football played by our teams. A short walk led to the new Pedagogic Institute, where we had permission to work in the spacious library.

One day of our six-day week was dedicated to military instruction. It seemed somehow unfair that female students and older students who had completed their military service were exempted. In the summer following our second year of studies, we had to present ourselves to the military barracks in Temeswar for basic boot camp instruction. Our civilian clothes were taken away and placed in storage. We received a set of military uniforms, boots, an infantry rifle and a gas mask. The large festive hall had been equipped with bunk beds and became our dormitory for the next month. At 5:30 each morning, we were awoken by the sound of a bugle. We had to be lined up in the courtyard by 5:55, dressed only in pants and boots, for our morning run. My most vivid recollection is an encounter with a platoon of Soviet soldiers, also out on their morning run. The Soviets were all athletic, or at least very well nourished, while our group looked more like a bunch of skeletons. Most of us were not surprised by the contrast: The Soviets were real soldiers, whereas we were just a group of students compelled to play soldiers.

The following two academic years were our last and we were back in the student residence located in the former hotel near Central Station. During the fifth year we were down to two students in a room, because we had reached the high status of seniors. Every room had a sink, but the water pressure was too low during the day, to bring the water up to the second floor. And there were not enough shower rooms in the building. But most important to me was that the building was free of bedbugs. From here it was only a short walk to the train station, which made my trips home to the village a lot easier.

We always walked from our student residence next to the Central Station to the lecture halls of our faculty, located in the building of the expropriated Piarists. Often we walked that distance twice in a day, sometimes even three times. During one of these walks, I experienced an unusual encounter that really shook me up, so that I could never forget it afterwards. Three people with their hands tied together were being escorted down the street by two militiamen. I immediately recognized the three prisoners; they were from Alexanderhausen. The older man was Mr. Lawrence, the grandfather of my friend Richard. Until the war came to our village, he had been the owner and operator of the largest general store in the village. He was known as an honest and kind man, always ready to help. I knew why they had arrested him and the two other people. Since they had no other options to make a living, they operated clandestine small shops in the village, they sold the products that they had purchased in Temeswar, such as matches and yeast, vinegar and safety pins. This minuscule illegal trade marked them as speculators and opponents of socialism. Mr. Lorenz looked like a very unhappy old man; you could see that he was on the verge of collapse. I turned my eyes away, hoping that he had not seen me.

The focus of my life had now shifted to Temeswar, but I still took the train back to the village every second or third weekend. Oma always found the ingredients to prepare some exceptional meals, as only she knew how. On these Sundays I took the opportunity to rest and recuperate, often by sleeping until lunch time. As I did during my commuting days, I returned to Temeswar on the early Monday morning train. Richard was in Jassy studying chemistry and came home rarely.

On a beautiful autumn Sunday I was invited to the wedding of a neighbour and distant relative. My partner for the walk to church and also for dinner was Helga. She was nice girl from a neighbouring village and attended high school in Temeswar. We enjoyed the food and wine, as we talked about everything under the sun and found that we held similar opinions on virtually all matters.

After midnight, I said my goodbyes because I wanted to sleep for a few hours, in preparation for yet another test on Monday. At the station I met Helga again, as she took the same train back to the city. As we sat together in the darkened compartment of the train, I put my head on her breasts as if attempting to sleep. When she bent her head down, I kissed her on the mouth. Not only did she let it happen, but she returned the kisses again and again. The time flew by so fast, that we reached the city before I could believe it. It was certainly the shortest of my many trips from Alexanderhausen to Temeswar.

During the following weeks, my thoughts often turned to Helga. Twice I walked past her boarding school, hoping to meet her by chance. I knew that I could ask the concierge of the boarding school to call her out. I even knew that this was really the only way to see her again, and so stay in touch. In the end, my imperative asserted itself again and I gave up on my attempts. Soon the many problems of daily life prevailed and Helga faded out to just a beautiful memory.

During the spring, fall and winter season, the State Opera of Temeswar presented a full repertoire of operas. I joined a group of five or six colleagues, all lovers of the opera. We had found out that a number of tickets were reserved for students. They went on sale every Monday morning, at a quite affordable cost. Our seats were located on the highest balcony, but that did not bother us in the least. We became quite familiar with the operas of Verdi and Puccini, but also with Eugene Onegin and Boris Godunov.

In a rather Viennese tradition, the operetta "Die Fledermaus" by Johann Strauss was presented on New Year's Eve. This was in the middle of our exams, but I often concluded that a break of that kind would do wonders for my endurance. I remember going there alone and staying on my seat during intermission. On a much lower balcony, a girl had also remained in her seat. We fixed our eyes on each other and smiled, repeatedly and for long times. In some sense it appeared that we had fallen in love and communicated without words. At the end of the presentation, I left the building by the side door reserved for my balcony, and headed straight for the main doors, where the girl would have to come out. I waited until the last person had come out, but the girl must have left earlier, so that I never saw her again.

# 19. STUDENT REVOLT

In the fall of 1956 all of us students followed the uprising in Hungary with great interest. There was much discontent among us students of the Polytechnic. The food in the student cafeteria was getting steadily worse. Twice a week we were served "mamaliga" (boiled corn flour, a type of corn bread or polenta) instead of the usual black bread. The only meat we saw were ears, tails and fatty remnants of the pig or sheep. I knew that many Romanian colleagues whose families were not affected by the expropriation, often found it very difficult to save the money for their student sons.

One day in that October, my turn came to serve as student delegate at our cafeteria. Together with a student from the Faculty of Chemistry, the assignment was to watch that all ingredients went into the kettles, and none were misappropriated by the personnel of the cafeteria. It was an almost impossible task, but we did what we could, as did all the other students when they served as student delegates. Around ten o'clock, there was really nothing more to monitor and we decided to go to the movies. The cinema was called "New Times" and it was conveniently located very close to our cafeteria, on the less-frequented side of the Corso promenade.

The student of chemistry was a cute little girl, a blonde with her hair tied up in a pony tail. We spent two pleasant hours at the cinema but came back in time before the cafeteria opened for lunch. In the following days, my imperative was once again put to a difficult test. Should I follow up on this emergent relationship or should I just drop it? Should I join the colleagues seen marching up and down in front of the residence for female students? Like so much in life, that would certainly have its advantages and its disadvantages. This time my decision was made easier by a series of external events.

A meeting in the Great Hall of the Faculty of Mechanical Engineering had been announced the day before. It was not clear to me who had called the meeting, but all students were invited and were supposedly encouraged to openly air their complaints. It seemed to me that the meeting would be an attempt by the party and government to probe the atmosphere among the students and perhaps to defuse it. That seemed to me a waste of time, and I avoid those staged meetings like the plague. At the six clock supper I met some classmates who were just returning from the meeting. They were obviously swept away by enthusiasm. Their consensus was that "Such a meeting takes place in Romania only once in a century".

What had happened? The representatives of the Party and Government had taken places on the stage and encouraged the students to speak freely. They were taken by the students at their word and the complaints and demands soon exceeded everything normally heard in this country. Gradually, the officials lost the conduct of the meeting to the students. When a student stood up and proposed "a moment of silence for the Hungarian people, which is fighting for its freedom," all the students stood up, but he officials left the stage in a hurry.

The students took over the conduct of the meeting and continued to work on the list of their demands. As it got closer to dinner time, a number of students, including my classmates, left the meeting. Others left for various reasons of their own. The students remaining in the hall did not notice that the building was being surrounded by some kind of army trucks. The men in uniform stormed the hall, arrested the students, and carried them away into the waiting trucks. The adjacent student residence was also raided by the army and the students captured were placed on the trucks. Some of the latter were dragged from their beds in their pyjamas. As the column of trucks began to move, no one knew where they were being taken. Soon the students were told that the military barracks in Kleinbetschkerek were their destination. There the students were handed over to the regular military, but nobody knew what would happen to them, not even their guards.

We returned to our student dorm near Central Station, and talked late into the night about the events of the day. The next morning I got up as usual, and with my towel wrapped around my neck, made my way downstairs to a bathroom on the ground floor where the water pressure was sufficient for the customary morning wash. Suddenly I heard a rough voice from the entrance hall: "Stop! Where do you think that you're going? Everyone stays in his room!"

In the hall, a machine gun was set up, with a full ammunition belt. Behind the machine gun was a man in uniform, and the hall was swarming with soldiers. The voice came from an officer who wore the uniform of a captain of the Air Force. He was clearly in charge of the operation. The soldiers were obviously Interior Ministry troops, and every student knew that they were the elite soldiers of the Securitate. The captain was wearing the uniform of the Air Force for reasons that only he knew, and that appeared somewhat mysterious to us students.

We were not allowed to leave the student residence, but no one could prevent us from opening some of the window facing the street leading to the railway station. From the passers-by, we learned that our colleagues were being held in the military barracks of Kleinbetschkerek. Among the workers passing by, many were commuters from the surrounding villages. Several of them asked us how we were doing and whether we needed anything. They said that they were ready to help us in every possible way.

When they brought us breakfast, no one touched it. The word "hunger strike" spread from room to room. Somehow we knew, or assumed, that the other students of the Polytechnic, those living in other student residences, were also on hunger strike. All of us wanted to ensure the release of our colleagues interned in Kleinbetschkerek. When lunch was brought in, no one touched it.

The day did not allow us to give any thought to our daily tasks and to the obligations of our study. We gathered in larger and smaller groups and discussed the big question: How can we and our colleagues extricate ourselves from this situation? Towards evening, the news spread that our colleagues in Kleinbetschkerek were being treated well and that some of them were already on the way back to the city. It was also said that our colleagues living in the other student dormitories had already enjoyed their dinner. The conclusion was that we had no valid reason to continue the hunger strike. When our dinner was brought in, we accepted it, but it did not taste quite right.

The following day, one of our professors appeared at our student residence. We gathered in the hallway and listened anxiously to his words. He did not blame us, but he reminded us that we should not prolong this unexpected free time too much, because the lectures and tests could hardly be rescheduled. All agreed with him and were relieved when he said that the lectures would restart on the next day. Before that, we all needed to sign a declaration to the effect that we would fully respect the constitution and the laws of the Romanian People's Republic. The declaration was passed around and every student put his signature next to his name.

Classes were indeed resumed the next day, after we were advised to walk on the street only individually and not in groups. On the way from the student cafeteria to the student residence, we walked only in twos, with a distance of ten paces between any two groups. Strangely enough, there were soldiers everywhere, walking around in twos or threes. They could not be overlooked as they were walking down the Corso promenade.

When the lectures were resumed, we noticed that two classmates were missing. They were the individuals who had spoken up at the meeting in the hall of the Faculty of Mechanical Engineering. They had complained bitterly about their living and studying conditions. Another colleague had managed to leave the meeting hall before the army stormed it. Because two colleagues claimed to be unable to identify him on some photographs, he was able to avoid further unpleasant consequences. Another colleague spent some time in the cellars of the Securitate. When he reappeared in the classroom, some colleagues asked him about his absence. He never gave an answer; he just turned around and walked away. He was subsequently admitted to write the tests and did not have to repeat the academic year.

Many years later, some people maintained that the meeting had been planned by a group of students from the Faculty of Mechanical Engineering, and not, as usual, by the comrades from the Party and government. Some far-reaching political demands are also being mentioned. At that time in October 1956, my colleagues and I never heard of such demands. I remember mostly the demands for better living conditions for the students and their parents. Each of us would certainly have liked to see the Russian occupiers gone home, and everyone wanted to have more personal and political freedom, as guaranteed on paper by the Constitution of the Romanian People's Republic. Many of us wanted freedom to travel, some of us even considering the idea of an escape to the West. But it was highly unlikely that many students believed that they could achieve a system change, or even a withdrawal of the Red Army from Romania. A return of the Banat to Hungary was not on the radar screen for the majority of students who were ethnic Romanians.

At that time, my colleagues would have shaken their heads in disbelief about such claims. Each of us wanted first and foremost to complete his studies successfully and stay out of the prisons maintained by the Securitate. If that group of students from the Faculty of Mechanical Engineering really envisaged higher goals, such as system change and others, they were certainly overestimating the power and influence of their relatively small group. Our students and professors had known for a long time that the party was sometimes considering the idea of dissolving the whole university centre of Temeswar.

One Saturday in October, I went home to the village and was surprised to find Richard there. During the night, Soviet tanks rumbled through the village, down the Szegedin highway. It was not hard to guess that they came from their depot in Temeswar and were on their way to Hungary. On Sunday morning we walked to the centre of the village, where half a dozen Soviet tanks had made a stop on the lawn behind the church. We looked at the tanks up close and commented on the rough welded joints. These machines had been made to bring death and destruction. In their design, aesthetics played no role. It was sad for us to know, that these tanks would reach Budapest the next day. We knew that they would brutally put down the Hungarian uprising. In the following days and weeks, we learned only after some delays, that the "counter-revolutionary, Western-directed coup in Hungary" had been successfully defeated.

In the summer we had to complete our military service, by playing soldiers again, this time for six weeks in Bucharest. It was a very hot summer, and we were thirsty all the time. Ice-cold water could be found only in a room of the officers' cafeteria. The water from the tap was always warm, good for showers but not for drinking. Our uniforms and boots were heavy, as were the rifles and gas masks. We practiced the basics of infantry tactics in the field during the morning, alternating with the tasks and procedures of military communications. The afternoon was spent mostly in a makeshift classroom, learning the theoretical foundations of military communications.

One Saturday the major in charge of our unit thought that we deserved a little rest and recreation. We marched in close formation to the football stadium. It so happened that the game was between the central team of the army and the team of the Temeswar Polytechnic. The latter was our team, and we shouted our support for it, as we did all year at its home games in Temeswar. But the fact that students in uniform were not supporting the team of the army was obviously interpreted as something close to mutiny by the guardians of public order. These guardians were troops of the Interior Ministry, and their leaders obviously felt extremely uncomfortable with this group of rebellious soldiers. They interpreted it as a protest or rebellion against the state, something that was simply not permitted in this country.

An officer of the security forces showed up and reminded us of our responsibility as members of the military. His efforts were in vain, as we continued to support our home team, just as we were used to do in Temeswar. We did not notice until it was too late, that Interior Ministry troops were slowly surrounding us. Once this encirclement was complete, an officer appeared with a few armed soldiers. They grabbed two of our supposed leaders and led them away. Then we were led out of the stadium and marched to our barracks through secondary streets.

Our Major said briefly that we had acted irresponsibly, and that we had embarrassed him. Our detained colleagues rejoined us a few days later in the barracks. If anybody asked a question about their whereabouts or their experiences, they gave no answer. An incident of a different type was caused by another colleague, when he visited us briefly in the barracks. He wore a fine suit and came from the World Youth Congress in Moscow. I had not even noticed his absence, because as president of the youth organization he usually followed his own agenda. Only later, back at the Polytechnic, I read in the student newspaper that he had been elected by us, his colleagues, to represent us in Moscow.

On the last day of our military service, we stood in the courtyard of our barracks and our officers stood in dress uniform before us. After a short speech by our major, about ten students were asked to step forward, including myself. We were congratulated and named as examples of well-prepared reserve officers. I felt most uncomfortable and imperceptibly shook my head in disbelief. Our officers were obviously not familiar with the documents sitting in the files of the personnel department.

After the start of the new year of studies, we were individually called to the office of the military department of our faculty, to review the official results of our completed military service. When it was my turn, the officer threw a glance at the documents and said: "What happened here? Is this a mistake?"

"Comrade major, this is not an error. My father lives in the West."

"Yes, that must be it" said the major, "I understand why are you still a sergeant."

It was the result that I had expected. The rank of reserve officer had no particular value for me, but as a sergeant I could now be called up for additional military exercises. If that happened, my superior could easily be one of those uneducated officers, who hated university graduates. There was only one real way out of this: emigration to the West.

## 20. An ending and a new beginning

As students in the fourth year of study, our student residence was again the expropriated hotel near Central Station. The food in the student cafeteria had improved somewhat and we even had our own student newspaper, published of course under the supervision of the Party. One Saturday I took the train back to the village. Oma took care of my belongings as always, perhaps even more than usual. Early Monday morning, I was getting ready to go back to Timisoara, as I had done so many times before. When Oma hugged me goodbye, she said: "My child, I wanted to tell you about my life, but I never got around to it."

I replied that I would love to hear it, and that we would have to catch up on that during my next visit. Later I blamed myself for not postponing my departure to listen to Oma's story. Such opportunities are rare in life, and they are so easy to miss. Oma put her arms around me again and said: "You must be strong, my child, promise me you'll stay strong!" With tears in my eyes, I assured her that I will never forget her advice. During the following days and weeks, whenever I remembered our farewell, my eyes filled with tears.

The next Wednesday was a busy day: lectures in the morning, laboratory work in the afternoon, clarification of some pending issues in the Central Library, dinner in the cafeteria next to the Corso. I returned late to the students' residence. The woman in service at the entrance gave me my room key and when I was already on my way to my room, she suddenly called me back:

"A man from your village left a note for you . . . but I can not find it anymore. Something about your grandmother . . . yes, I think she died."

What shocked me at first was the incredible indifference and carelessness of that woman. I went back and asked for the note; she kept looking for it, but could not find it. Once in my room, I tried at first to rationalize the indifference and negligence of the woman. To her, a family probably consisted of the children, the two parents, and the four grandparents. She could not know that the war had reduced our household to just Oma and me. Still less could she know that it was Oma, who had taken the place of my parents and had maintained the only home I knew for the last twelve years.

I had to think of our last goodbye, and knew immediately that Oma was no longer alive. My whole being rebelled against this conclusion, but I could feel that the impossible and unimaginable had happened. I knew better than anybody else, that her life had brought her a lot of work and many tears, but I also knew that her tireless efforts on my behalf and the things we achieved together gave her great satisfaction and much joy.

After a sleepless night, I took the morning train to the village, and walked toward our house, which until now had been my only real home. I stopped at Beckers, and they confirmed the sad news. Mrs. Becker said: "She sent for me and I immediately went to her. She lay in her bed and just wanted to say something. I leaned over and she said so softly that I could hardly understand: "Tell my boy, that for me he was everything I had in the world". Those were her last words. Then she peacefully went to sleep."

We went to our house where Oma was laid out in the big room. She had kept the last of the coffins made by my father for her own burial, because that was the easiest way. In the evening, many relatives, neighbours, friends, and some of Oma's friends came to the wake. Uncle Gerhard hugged me and cried, because he understood the insecurity and homelessness that had spared me until now, but suddenly appeared in my life.

The funeral took place next day, with a small choir of girls singing, but without music and without a stop in the church. That is how Oma wanted it: A simple funeral after a simple life. When I sat on the train that took me back to Temeswar, I was overcome by an immense fatigue, and I fought a sense of despair. I was confident that I would conclude my studies at the Polytechnic in the coming year. I had always imagined life after that: No more money worries for Oma or for me, a few good years for Oma, because she deserved them more than anybody else. That had long been a cornerstone of my plans for the future; now fate had once again decided otherwise. But I had promised Oma to be strong, and I was determined to keep this promise.

I spent the Christmas vacation of 1957 all alone in our house. Without Oma, it was empty and cold. With some help from the Beckers, I kept the big oven supplied with heating material. Many relatives, including Beckers, Uncle Gerhard and the family of my Uncle John invited me for dinner. They all did their best, but I missed the warmth of our own home and especially the presence of Oma. To maintain the house in the future, somebody had to live in it. In addition, I wanted to keep it in the family. Finally I sold the house to my Uncle Johann, the brother of my father. Grandmother, Uncle Johann, aunt Magdalena, and cousins Hans and Kathi moved in. I was pleased with this solution, because no one could know at the time that this part of the family would also leave for Germany in just a few years.

The following semester was entirely dedicated to my thesis. A trip to the factories in Reschitza had once again been scheduled. There I was able to spend time in the development office, where I followed the design and construction of various electric motors from conception to realization. I could direct my questions directly to their experienced engineers and learned a lot about the practical aspects of engineering. The work was new and interesting and I enjoyed it immensely. The work concentrated my thoughts toward my work, away from my personal predicament.

After returning to the student residence in Temeswar I continued the work on my dissertation. I did that work under the guidance and supervision of the dean of our faculty. At a joint review of the manuscript, we discovered an interesting but hitherto unnoticed aspect of the work. The dean saw my hesitation, and he knew that my colleagues had completed their dissertations long ago and were now enjoying their free time. He then asked me the question: "Let's say, Beethoven has just completed a symphony, when he has a new idea or inspiration. What would he do?"

I could not disappoint either the dean or Beethoven, so I agreed to continue working. I borrowed the compass set from my cousin Herman, and spent more time on my dissertation. I was counting on getting rewarded with the highest mark for my dissertation and I was not disappointed in the end.

After successfully passing the State Examination followed the all-important allocation of a permanent position in industry. We were asked to fill out a form, listing three desirable places, starting with the most desirable one. From then on it was not entirely clear what the procedure was. There was supposed to be some kind of a committee of professors and representatives of the student union that would try to match our listed preferences to the sites provided by the ministry. As far as we could find out, the criteria for matching the preferences to the sites available were based on the results obtained during the five years of study, as well as the "social activity" of the candidate.

I knew that my achievements were impressive. I reviewed all the marks obtained in the five years of study, as listed in my student book. There was not a single grade of "adequate", the mark of "good" appeared six times, but the top mark of "very good" stood there fifty times. Goose bumps ran down my spine as I looked back at it all: Fifty-six tests, fifty-six instances of exam anxiety, and fifty-six times the joy of success. A single failure, a single bad day, would have cost me my scholarship and would probably have meant the end of my studies.

But what exactly was meant by "social activity" and how and by whom was it evaluated? Like all students, I was a member of the student union introduced after the events of October 1956, but I had never joined the party or the union of young workers. The big question was, however, what weight did my father's stay in the West have? After the experience with my non-promotion by the military, I had little hope.

My dream would have been a position at a research institute, ideally located in our capital city of the Banat, Temeswar. But I was acutely aware that I did not have much hope of actually getting such a job. Like many classmates, I would have liked to have listed Temeswar three times as the desired locality when I filled out the questionnaire. Since that was not allowed, I had listed Temeswar, Arad and Lugosch as desirable places of work.

My final allocation was an engineering position at the city works of Arad. At the time, the village of Alexanderhausen belonged to the "rayon" (district) of Sânnicolau Mare (Großsanktnikolaus), which was part of the administrative region of Arad. Since Arad was the second largest city of Banat, even if it was not located on the Banat side of the river Marosch, I wanted to get to know the city. Moreover, I saw in this new situation some possible advantages for organizing my planned emigration.

I rented a room in one of the old houses on the main street of Neuarad. The water supply line of the city ended at a kind of pump just outside the house, where I filled my water jug every day. A convenient stop of the streetcar was also nearby. As an employee of the city works, I had a free ride on all streetcars and free access to urban baths.

My landlords were an ethnic German couple that had come from Russia many decades earlier. I reached an agreement with them, whereby I deliberately did not register my new address with the militia. We all knew that this was against the law, but I committed myself to pay any fines that they might incur because of this pretended negligence. Keeping my address in Alexanderhausen was an important part of my plan.

As a resident of Alexanderhausen I had to submit my application for emigration in Großsanktnikolaus. One morning I took the train from Arad to Großsanktnikolaus, went to the militia station, and filled out the application. I was determined that nobody would find out about this application, not in Alexanderhausen, and certainly not in Arad. My close friends knew that I wanted to emigrate, but they did not know anything about the concrete steps that I had taken.

My first job was as an engineer at the rectifier station, which supplied the streetcars with direct current. I met some experienced technicians, with whose invaluable help we were able to keep the mercury rectifier installation in operation. Later I was entrusted with a division of repair shops. I did my duty as I saw it, always in the hope of positive developments with my application for an exit visa. Meanwhile life had to go on, especially as I had now, for the first time in my life, overcome the chronic lack of money.

The months went by and out of Großsanktnikolaus came nothing but silence. In the fall I heard from my father that a Mr. Maurer of Montreal was about to visit his hometown Engelsbrunn. He gave me the exact date of the visit and I found Mr. Maurer in Engelsbrunn without difficulties. After a long, detailed conversation, I scribbled my thoughts on a piece of paper which Mr. Maurer handed my father on his return to Canada. It contained a summary of my efforts to leave the country and a plea for any possible assistance.

On a summer day of 1960, I was surprised by the arrival in Arad of my cousin Hans. He now lived in our house in Alexanderhausen and at the time was not actively contemplating emigration from Romania. On the previous evening, a local militia officer had knocked on the window. His message was that the militia in Großsanktnikolaus wanted to see him, and that it had something to do with his passport. My cousin was surprised, but the next morning he took the train to Großsanktnikolaus. There it soon became apparent that the militia actually wanted to talk to me, not to him. He took the first train to Arad and was now asking me about the meaning of it all.

We went for lunch to the best restaurant in Arad, and there I told him all about my plan. Each of us had heard of cases in which people had been fired from their jobs, once it became known that they had applied for leaving the country. Therefore I had kept my plan secret, even from him. He agreed wholeheartedly and promised me first, not to mention my application to anybody, and secondly, to let me know immediately if he received further news from the militia.

The next morning I boarded the train again in Arad and went to Großsanktnikolaus. A lieutenant of the militia put a sheet of paper into the typewriter and started asking me a large number of questions. It became obvious that the officer had the thankless job of recording the reason for my exit request.

"Comrade engineer, you were one of our good students and you have a good job. You recognize the great achievements of our socialist state?"

"I admire the great achievements of our country, but unfortunately I was left alone here as a result of the war, and now I would like to join what is left of my family."

"But you can do the same thing here at home. Ask your father to come back home."

"I've already done that several times. Since he was not wanted here right after the war, he has now established himself in the West and has given up on his home here. He says that it is my duty as his son, to join him. This is really the only way for me to ever see my father again."

And so it went, until the lieutenant ended the interview. He pulled the sheet of paper from his typewriter, read it to me, and I put my signature under it. I asked him if he could tell me something about the interview: Would he consider it a positive or a negative development? He said only that it proved that my file is obviously still under consideration, and has not yet landed in the trash can. That could only be considered positive. Some time passed, before Cousin Hans from Alexanderhausen reported that a stranger, a civilian, had come to the village and questioned several neighbours about me and my family. Since no one from our family could be described as an exploiter or class enemy, and since we had no known enemies in the village, we could assume that the investigation had gone well.

In my Arad office, I had a telephone call from a man with a somewhat unusual sounding Romanian name. He wanted to meet me at an address in a downtown building. He said that the purpose of the meeting was "a conversation in connection with your exit visa". Our conversation started with the same questions that had been asked by the lieutenant of the militia in Großsanktnikolaus. I tried my best to come up with the same answers. Then he proposed a follow-up meeting in the same apartment, about two weeks later. For that meeting, he asked me to jot down some comments about my boss, especially his weaknesses. My boss had received his degree a few years before me from the same university as I did, the Temeswar Polytechnic. Under no circumstances was I going to hurt him.

At our next meeting, which was thankfully also our last, I placed a small note on the table. In it I described my boss as a competent and conscientious engineer, but with the bourgeois habit of bringing a thermos filled with coffee to work. My interviewer did not pay any attention to the note at all. Instead, he put a blank sheet of paper in front of me and dictated a statement with roughly the following wording: "I (your name here) promise that I will not divulge to others my collaboration with the organs of the Securitate. If I break this promise, I shall suffer the severe punishment of the authorities of the Romanian People's Republic."

After I had signed that statement, I was allowed to leave. I thought for days about the purpose of the declaration I had just signed. Obviously it was not about keeping secret my cooperation, because no such cooperation had actually taken place. Was it an insurance policy against negative statements about the Romanian People's Republic that I could conceivably make in the future, or against possible attacks on the country and its government? Or was the declaration good enough to destroy my credibility, in case I should ever want to work for Western intelligence services? Since I had absolutely no intention to engage in any of those activities, I concluded that I did not have to worry about that declaration.

I could also see another possible purpose of this statement. If I were living in the West, then could the "authorities of the Romanian People's Republic" one day appear at my front door and ask me to cooperate with them? This possibility seemed so absurd to me, that I decided not to agonize about it any longer. When I think back about it today, I have to admit, that these meetings and the signed statement have contributed to the fact that I let nearly 25 years pass, before I set foot into Romania again.

I was next summoned to the regional militia headquarters in Temeswar. There a friendly lieutenant advised me, that my exit visa had been approved by Bucharest. Now he needed fourteen documents before he could officially issue my travel document. The approval was valid for six months, which left me enough time to obtain the necessary documents.

Shortly before, a Jewish engineer working with me at the company in Arad, had received his permission to leave. After he sold his belongings and gave up his apartment, the government suddenly decreed a ban on all departures to Israel. To avoid a similar fate, I submitted my resignation to the company immediately, and then devoted all my time to the gathering of the necessary documents.

I returned to the Temeswar militia two weeks later, equipped with the required fourteen official documents. To my disappointment, the confirmation obtained from my company, indicating that I did not owe anything, was rejected as incomplete. I went back to Arad for a last visit with my former company. The secretary of the director was kind enough to type a brand new document from a draft that I had prepared, and personally take it to the director for signature. He signed the certificate without saying a word and I was on my way.

Just before Christmas I held the long-awaited travel document in my hands. It was valid for six months so that I would not have to leave until May. I decided, however, to travel as quickly as possible, as soon as my father could arrange and pay for the airline ticket. I did not want to undertake the risk that the authorities would change their decision and revoke my travel document.

# 21. Saying goodbye

RC Church of Alexanderhausen

I wanted to spend Christmas with my relatives at our house in Alexanderhausen. Here I had spent the first ten years of my life with my parents and grandparents, and for those years I was grateful. Times were normal in those years and nobody would have been able to predict the events to come. I felt that it was my last Christmas in this house and in my home village, because I was literally sitting on packed suitcases. Of the people that once lived in this house, only my father and I were left, and he lived in a far-away country called Canada. Nearly seventeen years had passed since he had left for the Great War. The closer my great trip came, the less I could imagine the prospect of finally meeting my father again. The big wide world sometimes seemed like a great emptiness that had something unfriendly and threatening about it.

I was delayed in Arad from catching the train to Temeswar that would have allowed me to connect there to the evening train going to Alexanderhausen. The only alternative was to take the train to Großsanktnikolaus, via Perjamosch, get off at the Satu Nou stop, and somehow get from there to Alexanderhausen. When I got off the train at Satu Nou, there was no train going in the direction of Temeswar, for at least four hours. As I was carrying only a briefcase, I decided to walk towards Alexanderhausen on the railway tracks, as we had done in those now long-passed childhood years. The distance was barely over four miles, there was no snow on the ground, and the gentle wind did not really feel cold. The sun was hiding behind dark clouds, but the cornfields on both sides of the tracks looked eerie and even threatening. I had never seen these fields in the fall or in the winter, certainly not with the corn cobs still in place at this time of the year. All fields now belonged to the state, and the state had neglected to harvest its corn on time. I suddenly felt sad for the villagers who had to stand by and watch these fields, once their pride and joy, being left to the crows and to the rodents.

I joined my grandmother, my Uncle Johann, my aunt Magdalena, my cousin Hans and my cousin Kathi, now all living in our house. A bed had been set up for me, and I was always invited to dinner. The holidays brought further invitations and also the opportunity to say goodbye. Already in Temeswar I had purchased a camera from Soviet soldiers. I used it now to take group pictures with my relatives, friends and acquaintances. These shots were intended to keep the memory of my native village and its people alive in my future life.

In the house of the Becker family, the beautiful wall clock of my parents was hanging on a bedroom wall. Mrs. Beck mentioned that they wanted to keep the clock for me. Since my future now seemed to be in Canada, it was best if the clock remained in place until further notice. I handed over to the Beckers the proceeds of my house sale, a momentous decision that seemed to be the only correct one under the circumstances. They were going to ask their relatives in Philadelphia to let me have the equivalent sum in dollars. In this way, a considerable sum of money found its way from my father's side of the family to the relatives on my mother's side. No one could anticipate then, that the Beckers would leave the country in less than twenty years, and migrate to Mr. Becker's native village in Hessen.

My farewell from Uncle Gerhard took an interesting turn. Once more he described briefly his experiences in Russia during the October Revolution. There he found a people fascinated with the great ideas of freedom, equality and fraternity. Back in the village, he listened regular to the reports from Radio Moscow on the construction of the workers' paradise in the Soviet Union. His radical disillusionment occurred only when he experienced the real socialism of the postwar years. In the end, he summarized his experiences with the words: "You can tell your father that I am cured!"

During the following days I took more photos in the village, with the focus on the church and the war memorial. It was uncertain whether my road would lead me back to the village again some day or not. I wanted to keep the village in my memory the way it was at my departure. The possibility that in another three decades almost all my relatives, friends, neighbours and acquaintances would leave the village certainly never entered my mind.

I took a few extra days to say goodbye to my friends and colleagues in Arad. I had spent two youthful years there. Professionally, I was scarcely given the opportunity to apply even a small part of the knowledge acquired in five years at the Polytechnic. But I had left the lean student years, the period of saving and renunciation, completely behind me. I had male and female friends, and I recall that the red wine of Minisch was of a good vintage in those years.

My friends Martin, Michael and Bruno came along to celebrate my departure. All of them emphasized that they envied me, but they were happy that I had won the jackpot of those years: A visa to leave the country. I knew that each one of them, consciously or unconsciously, harboured the hope to emigrate to the West somewhere deep in his mind. At the time, there was not much hope, but sooner or later they would indeed all leave the Banat for the long journey to the West. Some of them had to wait another three decades until that time came.

Then cousin Hans arrived and we boarded the express train from Arad to Bucharest. Somewhere in Transylvania, a woman came into the compartment and brought in her luggage a horribly smelly cheese. Under normal circumstances I would have been very upset, but at the thought that the occurrence was really appropriate for a farewell tour, I could only smile.

Richard also wanted to come to Bucharest to say goodbye, but his work did not allow it. I called him from the North Train Station and he could barely hide his excitement about my upcoming trip. When Hans and I collected my tickets at the airline office, we learned that I was to take my suitcase to the airport for customs clearance the day before departure. That information could not be ignored as long as I was still in the country and wanted to avoid any possible obstacles in the way of my departure. Customs clearance did not take long. The contents of my suitcase were lifted piece by piece, and then dropped back. Everything was found to be in order.

The trip from the airport to the city took longer than expected and we still had a lot to do. To be able to take my engineering diploma abroad with me, it had to be registered by the Ministry of Education and its export to be approved by the Foreign Ministry. Everything went well at the Ministry of Education, and the Foreign Ministry quickly put its stamp on the diploma. Now we lacked the signature of a person that was not in the office and was not expected back until next day. All mentions of my departure next day received only one answer: "You can always send the diploma afterwards by mail." Neither of us had an excessive confidence in that method, but there was no other way out. Hans promised to pick up the diploma right after my departure at the Foreign Ministry and take it to the main post office. He would then send it by the best and most expensive way. It was all we could do, because I could not even consider the thought of postponing my trip, regardless of the consequences.

Early next morning we were back at the airport. At the entrance to the waiting room for international flights, we had to take leave, because no locals were admitted. Hans said: "You did it and I am very happy for you. Let us not loose hope that we will meet again some day!" We would actually have such a reunion, but it would be in Germany and after two dozen years.

I proceeded to a room in which a customs official was sitting behind a desk. As I stood alone in front of him, he asked me to empty all my pockets and put their contents on his desk. When that was done, he asked me if that was all, and I said yes. He flipped through my pocket calendar and stopped at a list of addresses. "What is this?" he asked and I answered:

"The addresses of my relatives and friends." With that, my customs check was done and I could proceed to the actual waiting room, and wait there for the call to board the aircraft. I was pleasantly surprised, because I had expected a close body search, possibly even with undressing. It was obvious that the holders of passports were treated better than the ordinary inhabitants of the country.

## 22. Departure

Finally it was time for departure. The roar of the propellers reached a crescendo and the airplane lifted itself into the morning sky over Bucharest. After a few course corrections, it set a firm course westward. Only half of the seats were occupied. I looked at my fellow passengers. Most of them were Western business travelers, owners of real passports. These were the exotics that we always regarded as demigods, because neither the border nor the Iron Curtain, both impenetrable for us, represented an obstacle for them.

It was my first flight and it crossed a few borders. I had no real passport, just a travel document, valid for a single exit. There was no going back, even if I wanted it for some unknown reason. I had not joined the demigods; I was just a stateless expatriate, but I felt like I was in the seventh heaven. I had really won the first prize in the emigration sweepstakes and I was free to travel to the West, into the great wide world. It was the dream of many, but for most of them it remained only a dream.

At some point we crossed the Banat, my former world, the world of my childhood and youth. The thoughts rushed through my mind. There was the village of my childhood, my home for fifteen years. There was our beautiful city of Temeswar, where I had spent ten years as a student, years full of sacrifices, but wonderful years nevertheless. I thought of all the people who had played roles in my first twenty-five years, those still living and those who had already left this world. A period of my life was ending, a youth filled with hardships, which still had left me with so many beautiful memories.

Tears came into my eyes. I thought about the path I had traveled, the path from child to adult. Fate had imposed so many tests on me, but I had finally passed them all. I had seen tears everywhere and at all times; they were the companions of our life. So much of our world was doomed and had to die, and it weighed heavily on the mind.

The time had come to draw a line under this past and to make room for a new life. The future confronted me like a big question mark. But in stark contrast to the past, it contained some justifiable hope for a better life.

# 23. Arrival

The flight attendants on board the Boeing 707 were young, pretty and smartly dressed, and they spoilt us with good food and drinks, so that the time passed very quickly. After a flight of about seven hours, the aircraft prepared for landing in Montreal. I already had experienced three landings, all in a small propeller plane. This time it was a big jet plane, but we had little time to get scared, because with a barely perceptible jerk the plane landed on the runway.

I had filled out the customs declaration in English and expected the questions of customs officials. They actually searched my suitcase and confiscated the piece of ham, which Mrs. Beck had put in my suitcase as a special treat for my father. I had just learned an important lesson: In order to prevent the introduction of diseases, Canada did not allow any private importation of food.

The officers of the Canadian Immigration Service processed the regular travellers before us immigrants. I had to fill out an immigration card, in English or French. In this card I entered the German version of my first name and last name, as shown on my birth certificate, but not on my travel document. I was pleasantly surprised that the correction of my name was done so easily and efficiently. I was handed the bottom portion of the immigration card, with the instruction to take good care of it, because that was now my identity card. In addition to my name, it contained the stamp of the airline, as well as the stamp of the Canadian Immigration with the signature of its official. Now I had officially acquired the status of a "landed immigrant". I was now a legal resident of Canada, but I had to wait five years before I could apply for citizenship.

I walked toward the exit and could immediately make out my reception group of compatriots. Even after seventeen years, I recognized my father immediately. It was more difficult with some of the others. I recognized Mr. Maurer because I had met him some fifteen months before in Engelsbrunn. I even recognized the Schwarz family, but my former friend and classmate Robert Kremling had to actually introduce himself by his name; he had changed a lot while growing up. There were countless hugs and a few tears. Then we all stepped into the parked cars for the journey through the city.

It was early March and an ice storm had hit the huge city of Montreal the day before. What I could see of the landscape looked pretty bleak. As we drove through several suburbs, I could see the taller buildings of the city centre only as a shadow in the distance. I could distinguish some ten- or twelve-story brick buildings, but there were still no skyscrapers.

We reached the residence of my father in Montreal North and sat down for a snack. All those present accompanied the snacks with several glasses of my father's white house wine, until we were all in a pretty good mood. There was so much to tell, and I did my best to answer the many questions put to me. I found out soon enough that the events that had occurred in the Banat after 1944 were incomprehensible to those who had not lived through them. It was late in the evening, when our compatriots left for their homes.

It was only now that my father told me the story of his survival during the last days of the war. His unit was lucky to get on one of the last ships transporting army units from the Narva region to mainland Germany. With its few motorized vehicles and small pieces of artillery, the unit was moving westwards, ahead of the pursuing Red Army. My father was responsible for the remaining ammunition carried on their trucks. When they arrived in a village, the ammunition had to be unloaded and stored separately. When they got back underway, the ammunition had to be loaded back on the trucks. One morning they had to leave a village in a hurry, because the Soviet troops were entering the village from the other end. In the panic, the ammunition was left behind. When the officer in charge of the unit realized that the ammunition was missing, he accused my father of neglect of duty. He threatened him with a military court that would most likely condemn him to death. Luckily, they crossed the Elbe River before that could happen, and surrendered to the British. Without exception, the men considered themselves lucky to have avoided capture by the red Army, an event considered equivalent to a death sentence.

I slept on the sofa in the living room where the family TV was also located. It was a black and white TV and the screen had rounded corners, but it was certainly a step forward from my apartment in Neuarad, where all I had was a radio. On one of the following evenings I watched a hockey game before going to bed. When the game degenerated into a wild brawl on the ice, I turned off the set and went to sleep. I remember distinctly that I had some violent dreams.

I was very eager to get to know my new hometown as quickly as possible, so I was glad to participate in the weekly family trip to the supermarket. Everything was available in abundance, just as I had expected it from a food store in the West. The difference between the society of scarcity that I had just left and this affluent society was overwhelming. Even the concept of self-service was new to me: Every buyer pushed his cart and helped himself to the merchandise of his choice. How was it possible that people did not put anything into their own pockets? The best explanation seemed to be that the prices were low and that people had money. Was that not the best definition of a society that took the needs of its people seriously? I was surprised that ready-to-cook chickens cost thirty cents a pound (half a kilo) and a family of three could buy enough groceries for a whole week for about 20 dollars.

Buses provided the only public transportation in Montreal at the time. To get to the city centre by a bus, I had to change buses twice and the whole trip took longer than an hour. To me, the city centre was the main shopping street commonly called Saint-Catherine Street, and later officially called rue Sainte-Catherine. Here I found the huge department stores, with their seven or eight storeys. Their ads claimed that they carried everything you needed, "from the cradle to the coffin." I could hardly afford any of these goods, but I was certainly free to admire them.

One day there was a telephone call from a Mrs. Zukerman. I had left local currency worth about 100 Dollars with her relatives in Arad. Mr. and Mrs. Zukerman visited us the next day. As they sat on our sofa, Mrs. Zuckerman said to her husband: "Do you remember that we had a sofa just like this, when we had just arrived in Canada." We talked about her family and life in Romania, then Mr. Zukerman handed me ninety Canadian Dollars and the couple left. It was just a little pocket money, but I was glad that I could now continue my little bus trips to the city for a while longer. For the princely sum of four Dollars I bought Langenscheidt's Pocket Dictionary English-German and German-English. It still stands on my bookshelf today.

During the following weeks I was waiting for the postman every day and was always disappointed when my diploma was not among the arriving mail. After six weeks of waiting, it finally arrived intact and restored my trust in the international postal service.

Once when I walked down Saint-Catherine Street West, in the direction of the ice hockey stadium called Forum, I passed a grocery store. Suddenly the door opened and a man ran into the street, followed by two police officers with guns drawn. The three men ran past me, even before I had time to get scared. I looked around for a camera crew, but none was around. This was no film shot; it was a real, if not exactly everyday, scene from the life of the city.

## 24. THE NEW HOUSE

My father had moved from England to Canada to get married for the second time. His wife Anna was from Alexanderhausen and had lost her husband in the war. Like my father, she had reached her fortieth year and did not want to live alone. Anna had a daughter called Ann, which is the English form of Anna. Ann was married to a Romanian named Demetrescu, who was fluent in German and called himself Mr. Demet. That abbreviation was easier for most Canadians to pronounce without difficulty. When I arrived in Montreal, Mr. Demet and Ann lived in a rented apartment in a suburb called Park Extension.

After several weeks, both families moved into a brand new house. The building was known as a duplex: Two apartments above each other, each apartment having four rooms, a kitchen and a bathroom. The downstairs apartment had direct access to the finished basement: a large game or entertainment room, a bathroom and a one-car garage. Anna, my father and I lived upstairs, while Mr. Demet and Ann lived downstairs. Since each of the two families had paid half of the purchase price, they supposedly shared equal access to the basement.

My room had a large window facing the street. From the furniture factory that employed him, my father obtained a large desk for my room. A compatriot from the Banat, who owned a furniture store in Montreal, sold me a simple bed and a chair to go with my new desk. It was understood that I would pay for it later, after I had earned some money. At Woolworths I found a dirt-cheap little night table. On it I placed a homemade lamp, made from a large Chianti bottle with a switch and bulb holder combination mounted in a cork. The lamp shade included a wire frame which was placed directly on the light bulb. Now I was able to read in bed, and I was happy to do so every night before falling asleep.

Later on I added a radio to the small night table and a set of bookshelves built of boards and bricks. That type of improvised bookshelf would become quite typical for the hippie generation of the late nineteen-sixties.

There was so much to read, German and English newspapers, magazines and books. At the beginning, I always kept my Langenscheidt dictionary handy when reading the local English newspapers.

Eventually I enrolled in a language course "English for Beginners" at the local McGill University. At the very first lesson I was promoted to the next level, called "Intermediate English". Since at home we spoke only the Schwowisch dialect of Alexanderhausen, plus German and Romanian with Mr. Demet, my first extended conversation in English with a native Canadian was actually a kind of job interview in the offices of Canadian Immigration.

Before I left Romania, the local newspapers had reported about eight percent unemployment in Canada. I did not take that message verbatim, and was convinced that whatever this percentage was, it could not possibly apply to the subgroup of engineers. Now I found, to my dismay, that the economy was actually in decline, and that most firms were reducing the number of their employees. I borrowed Ann's typewriter and typed a large number of job applications. I sent them to various companies, whose addresses I had taken either from the local newspaper or from the telephone book.

The result was completely unexpected and incomprehensible at the same time. Most companies did not answer at all, while others sent form letters, in which they claimed to be very impressed with my qualifications, but unfortunately did not have any job vacancies. Often they concluded with the words: "Do not call us; we will call you when a job becomes available."

One day Mr. Demet invited me for a car ride. I thought at first that he wanted to give me driving lessons, because at some point in the near or distant future, I was certainly going to buy a car. Instead, he parked the car next to a small park and solemnly declared that he wanted to talk to me. He explained that the two families had bought the new house in order to give me a nicer home at a better address, but they also counted on my help with the monthly payments. In other words, I should begin to pay my 100 dollars a month for room and board. All I could say was that I had tried everything possible to get a job, so far without success. Should I really start as a dishwasher, as so many wealthy Canadians and Americans claimed in their biographies? No one was unhappier about my involuntary unemployment than I was myself. But I had finally joined my father after seventeen years of separation, and I assumed that I could count on his patience until I found a job. Mr. Demet ended the conversation with the admonition that I had to step up my efforts to find a job. He strongly suggested that I should personally visit some companies and ask for a job. I had to reject this suggestion as unreasonable. If a company had no vacancies, it would certainly not create one, just because an immigrant showed up in person at their doorstep.

I found that the social isolation, the lack of close friends of both sexes, made life very difficult. That loneliness rested heavily on my shoulders especially during holidays and long weekends. My homesickness and my dismal mood are reflected in some verses that I wrote in my diary just before my first Christmas in Canada:

On the shores of the St. Lawrence
An endless sea of houses,
Homes to two million people
Yet I find it cold and bare.

People rushing in the morning
Out to their important work,
Returning late in the evening,
Very late the lights go out . . .

Silently in the evening sky
Rests the same moon we once found.
Across lands and ocean
All my thoughts are homeward bound . . .

I cannot explain why this page of the diary has survived; I am actually quite surprised about it. Soon after starting my diary, once I started working, there was no time left for nostalgic thoughts and past-oriented verses. By then my initial difficulties were over and I did not want to be reminded of them by a diary. After I had torn out the page with the verses, the rest of the diary became a victim of the flames in the fireplace.

# 25. Finding a job

Within the Canadian Immigration Office on Dorchester Boulevard, there was an employment office dedicated to helping immigrants find jobs. I had already obtained an official translation of my engineering diploma, certified by a notary. With this paper in my pocket, I went to see the officer in charge of the recruitment of professionals. He took one quick look at my paper and sent me to a private company also located on Dorchester Boulevard. There I had a friendly conversation with a Mr. MacGregor. He ended up asking me if I had a car. When I said that I had none, he said that he was sorry, because the two vacancies known to him were located out of town, and could only be reached by car.

The local newspaper published very few openings for engineers, and virtually all of them demanded two years of Canadian experience. But how could an immigrant acquire this experience, if not through work? About a week after the conversation with Mr. Demet in his car, I went back to the employment section at the Canadian Immigration, and was sent back to Mr. MacGregor. He informed me once again that he was aware of some open positions for young engineers, located outside of the city limits. He did not tell me how I could have acquired a car in the meantime.

My father mentioned my difficulties with finding a job to the owner of the furniture factory where he worked. The owner offered to help. One of his relatives owned a small factory that produced components for larger companies. The little factory was equipped with a turning shop, a workshop for electrical work and probably a small technical department. I was told to just show up there on a Monday morning and somebody would take care of me. There I was indeed received by the foreman of the electrical shop, who had apparently been informed that I would show up, but had no idea what to do with me. He gave me a few little things to do and advised me to always look busy. But as I was wearing my one and only street suit and had no appropriate work clothes, I was certainly conspicuous. I went there for two more days, but did not get to see the owner. After the failures experienced in my previous job hunting, I did not have the confidence to track down that invisible boss. If he really wanted to see me, he would have either called me into his office or he would have come down to the workshop. On the fourth day I stayed home and explained that I could not go on like this. If I could not find suitable work in Canada, I was ready to consider moving to Germany. My father vetoed this option, leaving me no choice but to continue my job search. I was careful to go out of Mr. Demet's way, because I wanted to avoid another car ride with him at all costs.

It was in August that I found in the local German-language newspaper an offer for a position in a small company that manufactured small diesel-generator sets to the specifications of its customers. I called the company and was immediately invited for an interview. Its owner and chief engineer was a Greek-Canadian. When I sat facing him in his office, my eyes fell on an M. Eng. (Master of Engineering) degree from McGill University in Montreal, framed under glass and hung on the wall. After a quite reasonable conversation, he handed me the specifications for a diesel-generator unit to take home and study, so that we could discuss it the following Monday.

On Monday I was back on time, prepared to have a good discussion of those specifications. The owner asked me only if I had understood the requirements and if I was confident that I could contribute to the development of these units. I answered with an enthusiastic yes, because I felt that my unemployment was finally coming to an end. When he asked me about my salary expectations, I made the mistake typical of a greenhorn: I said that I would leave that entirely up to him. He went on stressing that many things are done differently here in Canada, so that I had an extensive training period ahead of me. Then he leaned back in his chair and said: "How about two hundred dollars a month to start? Later on it could, of course, be much more." It was really very little, far less than the current rate of pay for young Canadian engineers. Since I had to pay half of it for room and board, I would be left with only one hundred dollars a month. He must have noticed my disappointment, for he added: "If you find something better later on, you can accept it any time." I accepted his offer and started working the next morning.

The development team consisted of six people. Five of them were immigrants, and the sixth was a French-Canadian. We selected suitable units according to the needs of each client, which were chosen from a catalog, then assembled and tested on the factory floor. I was amazed that even the workers in the factory were all immigrants.

As our design department was only separated by a door from the office of our chief engineer and business owner, one day we overheard a conversation between him and a customer. Our boss tried to convince his customer that his company could only make a profit through the employment of immigrants. The Canadian Immigration Department sent him the prospective employees directly from the ship or airport, before they could get orientated about working conditions and wages in the country. Most left the company after a few months, or a few years at the latest, once they had learned English and found better paying jobs. Our boss presented a convincing case that this was not exploitation, but simply help to immigrants.

After a couple of months, my daily routine had become almost a habit. A half-hour bus ride to the company, eight hours in the office, then another half-hour bus ride home. The work was not strenuous and I was still learning something, both in terms of language and profession. When I returned home one evening, I found a message that somebody wanted to talk to me about a job. I remembered that I had filled out an application form at that office a few months before. At first I ignored the call, because I did not want to change jobs after less than three months on my current job. A few days later, the telephone rang again during our dinner. The same individual asked me if I had a job, and if I was satisfied with it. When I answered both questions in the affirmative, he asked me if I could indicate to him the approximate range of my salary. This was extremely unusual, because I knew that salary information was kept strictly secret in North America. When I said that I was earning less than 300 dollars a month, he said: "You should really come in for an interview, because I have an offer for a position that could pay you at least 600 dollars a month."

This was an offer that I could not easily reject. After all, I had debts and also wanted to take something to the bank after every payday. The next day, right after work, I took a bus to the office of the insistent caller. His company was hiring engineers and technicians for the Montreal branch of a large American engineering firm. He ordered a taxi and we drove to the headquarters of the engineering office. In the taxi he asked me how long I had been in Canada, and I answered truthfully: "For ten months." He replied that no one would believe me, and my answer to that question should be: "For nearly two years."

Soon we were sitting across from the head of the department of electrical engineering. Mr. Blinn was a nice older American and the conversation proceeded in a friendly tone. I was glad that he did not ask me about the length of my stay in Canada. After the two men had consulted for several minutes, the recruiter told me that I could start Monday. My salary was 620 dollars a month and was initially paid by the recruiting company. After about six weeks, Mr. Blinn asked me to join the engineering team of his company as a permanent member. I was happy to accept the proposal, even if a pay increase was only envisaged for a later date. This was my first permanent job in the New World, and it even brought some social benefits with it.

The work was new and interesting. We developed the complex motor control system of a fully automated factory for the concentration of iron ore. The factory was under construction in the far north, at Wabush-Labrador City. Our schematic drawings were flown by plane directly to the construction site, where electricians used them to wire the motor control cabinets. My group leader, a Lithuanian, was an expert in this field and I had much to learn from him.

In autumn 1962 I bought my first car: a brand new eight-cylinder Chevrolet Impala. It was large enough to easily accommodate six or seven passengers. At the time, safety belts were not yet in use. The engine certainly wasted gasoline, but at about 30 cents a gallon (4.5 litres), gasoline was really cheap. By car I could be in my office in ten minutes, while people were often waiting longer than that for a bus. To continue my education, I enrolled at McGill University for an evening course on feedback control systems.

On a work-free Saturday morning in February I woke up around eight o'clock and turned on the radio. In the local news somebody was reporting from a fire at a company located in the west end of the city. After a while it became clear that the fire was at our engineering firm. I skipped breakfast, jumped in my car and drove in the direction of the company. The police had blocked some streets in the area, so that I had to park the car nearby and continue on foot. On the way I met some colleagues and we were all very excited and anxious about our engineering documents and our jobs.

During the following week, the company rented a large hall and provided us with copies of the latest version of our documents, as they could find them at the construction site. Because these were undergoing constant revision and, in addition, new electricians had been hired at the construction site, soon nobody knew exactly which documents had actually been used to wire the motor control cabinets. The company's management decided to send a group of young engineers and technicians to Wabush, to clarify the situation on site. I volunteered for this mission before I was appointed.

On his arrival in Wabush, our plane had to circle the runway a few times before the landing gear could be properly deployed. The temperature was about—48ºC when we took possession of our cars. Four of us shared a car, and I was pleased that two members of my group volunteered as drivers, because the roads were covered with a permanent layer of uneven ice.

Our living quarters were some trailers parked not very far from the construction site. Each trailer was equipped with a continuously running gas heater. We took turns in the morning, to go out in the cold and plug in the electric heaters built into the cars. This had to happen at least half an hour before our departure, and even then the car windows were barely thawed out when we started driving. We had to drive to the cafeteria for breakfast. We left the car engine running during breakfast, so that the car windows were finally free of ice for the trip to the construction site.

From the outside, the factory looked as good as finished. Inside the building there was a temperature by 25ºC, so we had to take off our wool jackets to do our work. Each of us stepped inside of one of the relay cabinets and made a sketch of the relays and the actual wiring of their contacts. Every hour our sketches were taken to the drafting office, so that the draftsmen could incorporate them into the correct drawings.

We completed our work in two weeks and then took the airplane back to Montreal. The weeks of winter in the far north soon faded back into memory. It had been an interesting experience overall, but the food in the cafeteria reminded me of my military service in Temeswar and Bucharest. I failed to understand how the allegedly different preparations always produced the same end result: All meals had the same taste, or rather very little taste.

In the fall, the plant was successfully commissioned and our work on it was completed. Our engineering company was bidding on other major contracts, but was only able to get smaller projects. We received our salaries every other week, in the form of a cheque in an envelope. On every payday, some colleagues found in their pay envelopes a lay-off letter printed on pink paper. Our paydays were now more eagerly awaited than ever: Who would get a pink slip this time?

My group leader had also left and had found a new job in the city centre. From there he called me every few days, described his interesting new major contract and wanted to know when I was ready to join him. The biweekly layoffs continued, and one day I went to talk to Mr. Blinn. I told him that I had received a good offer from another company and was looking for his advice on whether I should stay or leave. His answer was that he did not want to lose me, but that he could not guarantee anyone's job. After all sorts of considerations over weekend, I came to the conclusion that it would be better to get rid of the uncertainty. The following Monday I submitted my letter of resignation and spent my last two weeks at this company doing very little work.

## 26. The next step

In downtown Montreal, between Saint-Catherine Street and Dorchester Boulevard, a 47-story skyscraper was completed in 1962. The new building, with its cross-shaped cross section, was called Place Ville-Marie and was the most striking building in the city. My new office was located on the 24th floor of that skyscraper.

Our section of the engineering firm was working on a new process for the production of aluminum, under contract to the large company Alcan, which was then the largest Canadian producer of aluminum. The process was experimental and therefore was kept secret, but we knew that it represented a low-cost alternative to electrolysis.

Once again, our group was engaged in the development of the motor control system. My job was to review the schematics before my boss officially released them to the construction site. With the increased responsibility came a higher salary. Since I drove to work by car, I had to pay for parking in the garage of the Canadian National Railway. In those days, the fee for parking was only twenty dollars per month.

We soon got used to the fact that we were working with the city at our feet. During thunderstorms or strong winds, it could get just a little scary, even though the actual movement of the skyscraper could not be perceived directly. On sunny days, however, and even when the snow fell, the view of the city was truly beautiful. I often talked to a nice French-Canadian secretary working in an adjacent office. I was still too much an immigrant, unsettled and lacking the stability to enter into a relationship.

One Friday in November 1963 the news electrified the entire building, including our office, that President Kennedy had been assassinated in Dallas. Everybody was shocked and little work was accomplished that day. People were standing around in groups, trying to understand the incomprehensible. It was particularly difficult for me and the other immigrants from the communist countries. We had experienced terror, persecution and lawlessness, but never the assassination of a head of state.

When spring came, some colleagues started receiving those pink slips in their paycheck envelopes. The rumour was that the completion of the new aluminum processing system had been postponed and only a few engineers and technicians would be needed to keep the documentation up to date.

A year earlier I had sent a job application letter to a company named Telecom. The company was a leader in Canada in the field of telephone switching and transmission technology. It manufactured and installed telecommunications equipment, from telephones to telephone exchanges, and from cable and wireless systems to radio communication systems. I had almost forgotten about this application, when I received a written invitation to a job interview. After confirming an appointment by telephone, I went to the office they had specified. It was actually located on Saint-Catherine Street West, not far from the Place Ville-Marie complex. I was offered a position as a systems engineer in the area of power supply to telecommunication systems.

After several days of consideration, I accepted the offer of employment, despite its slightly lower salary. In this way I moved into a new area of activity, which presupposed the willingness to learn new things. The rapid development of semiconductor technology had brought many innovations to the telecommunications sector. How far these new technologies would impact telecommunications could not yet be assessed. One thing seemed perfectly clear to me: I now had a stable job that was not dependent on new contracts or contract extensions. I joined a large and successful company in the telecommunications industry, which was planning a dramatic expansion of its areas of competence. The company continued to hire engineers, and I could expect more stability in my professional life. I had left the days of frequent job changes behind me.

## 27. Old Canadians and New Canadians

Some of our countrymen from the Banat had come to Canada before the Second World War and we referred to them as Old Canadians. Others had arrived only after the Second World War and we called them New Canadians. In the 1940s some of our Old Canadian acquaintances had become the owners of their own businesses. Now they were able to offer jobs in their factories or workshops to some of the New Canadians. The owner of the furniture factory in which my father and many other compatriots found work, was the son of immigrants from the Banat. The owner of another small company in which I worked for a grand total of three days, was also an Old Canadian. I never met him, but he certainly made his contribution to my difficult start in the new country.

A more or less typical Old Canadian was Mr. Maurer, whom I had met during his visit to Engelsbrunn. Since he was a good friend of my father, we visited him soon after my arrival in Montreal. Some compatriots claimed that he owned some 14 apartment buildings in Montreal and was the richest Danube Swabian in the city. He had arrived in Canada from Engelsbrunn in the 1920s. Like many other Banaters, he spent his first years in an apartment on De Bullion Street and took any job he could get. After a while, he specialized as a house painter and worked seven days a week. He was fond to tell the story about a Sunday morning, when he was pulling his little cart with the paint cans and brushes, through the streets of downtown Montreal. A group of Banaters standing in front of St. Bonifatius Church were laughing at him and commenting: "There goes the stupid Maurer, working on a Sunday."

But Mr. Maurer was one of the first to buy a car, ensuring that he never had to pull a cart with his painting utensils. Eventually he was able to buy a small, decrepit house in the city centre, for an affordable price. After a time, he converted the house into a small apartment building with six apartments. There he lived first as owner and caretaker, until he moved with his family into a brand new single house located outside the city centre. In this house we visited the Maurer family and had many interesting discussions. After several glasses of wine I asked Mr. Maurer if he really was the richest of our countrymen. He replied only that he was certainly carrying the highest debt. Before a building was fully paid, he had to buy another one, so that the taxes would not eat up any profit. The gradual acquisition of the houses was made possible only through ongoing mortgages from his bank.

During our visit, the phone rang about once every hour. The callers were residents of the various apartments, who had various problems such as broken windows, burned-out light bulbs, overflowing toilets. Mr. Maurer always found the right soothing words, coupled with the promise that everything would be fixed the next day. He had obviously become accustomed to these calls and did not find them annoying. When he told me, however, that someone with my intelligence and education could make a living "just on the phone" I had to truthfully say that I would rather go to the office every day and sleep undisturbed during the night.

Just like the Old Canadians, New Canadians generally did not like the idea of paying rent. They looked at the rental payments as money thrown away, because they left nothing tangible behind, nothing that they could call their own. To avoid these payments, the families saved money and when they had enough for a down payment, they bought a house and moved in. The houses bought were often duplexes (buildings with two apartments) or triplexes (buildings with three apartments). The family moved into one of the apartments and rented out the other or others. The collected rental payments were generally sufficient to cover the monthly repayments of the mortgage to the bank. After twenty or twenty-five years, the building came debt-free into the possession of our countrymen. The rental payments collected from now on represented their retirement income, since the owners of these houses often did not receive any pension from the government or from their previous employers.

To me, Peter Schwarz was the archetype of these successful countrymen. Early on, before my arrival in Canada, he had bought a triplex in one of the developing suburbs. There I visited him many times. In the beginning, when I still had no car, he picked me up with his car and brought me home again afterwards. The Kremling family also lived nearby, so that Robert was often able to join us. Then we drank a few beers and talked about our childhood in the Banat, and the trials and tribulations of fate that had reunited us here in Canada.

Peter had been severely wounded in the last months of the war and the end of the war found him in Germany. In a refugee camp in Austria he met his parents who had fled from the Banat. There he also fell in love with a girl from the Banat village of Dreispitz. After the two married and had their first child, they considered their prospects in Austria unfavourable, and decided to immigrate to Canada. Peter's parents joined them on the trip.

Robert had also survived several refugee camps before his family decided on emigration to Canada. His education had started in Germany and was interrupted by his departure. In Canada, he had acquired various vocational skills and was working as a technician. We often played table tennis and talked a lot about operas and their composers.

On a weekend in the fall, Peter and Robert invited me to accompany them on a hunting trip to northern Quebec. The car, with four-wheel drive, was fully loaded with all sorts of provisions, rifles, ammunition, food, and a few boxes of beer. North of the town called Sainte-Agathe we left the highway and drove right through the forest, or "bush", as it is called here. Peter knew the way by heart and we arrived at the hunting lodge late in the afternoon. As it was too late for hunting, we sat around the campfire, roasting our "gypsy bacon" and washing it down with beer. Next morning we climbed on our hunting stand, each of us with a loaded rifle. Unfortunately, no deer, bear, fox or wolf showed up. Perhaps the animals knew how much firepower was aligned against them. Some of Peter's hunting trips were more successful and I had the opportunity to taste the meat of the American elk, which is actually called a moose on this continent.

Peter's parents, Anton and Theresia Schwarz, had moved from Montreal to the country. They had bought a small farm in the Eastern Townships (Cantons de l'Est) located east of Montreal. Anton wanted to try farming once again, although this time around he was not interested in maximizing his income or buying more land. He knew very well that he was too old for commercially developing the farm. I remember a visit to the farm, with Peter and Robert. We had placed bottles and pots as targets on a fence and practiced target shooting with a couple of rifles. Then we were offered a few glasses of wine and concluded that Anton had the best wine of all our compatriots. He used grapes imported from California, just like our countrymen in Montreal, but he had a proper cellar. A door that seemed to open up into a hill, actually led to a cellar, the temperature of which changed little over the seasons.

After a few years, Anton and Theresia sold the farm and moved back to the city. They bought a small house not far from the bungalow in which Peter and his family were now living. Even Peter's parents-in-law were living in this suburb, where they owned another triplex. In the 1970s, after the parents and in-laws had left this world, Peter inherited two houses and was now the owner of three fully paid homes. In the late 1970s, when the nationalist movement in Québec caused some unrest that led to a decline of the economy, Peter sold the three houses and moved to Toronto. There he bought a house for his family and a rental property with sixteen apartments. He had become independent in his old age and did not have to rely on either private or government pensions.

Many of our countrymen from the Banat acquired not only their own houses, but also rental property which provided them with a steady income in their old age. They had lost everything when they had to leave the Banat at the end of World War II. But through their hard work, thrift and perseverance, they had managed to recreate a secure livelihood for themselves and their families. As their relatives and friends left behind in the Banat found out about these successful new beginnings, their resolve to leave their ancestral homeland could only be strengthened.

# 28. THE VAST COUNTRY

Some families from Alexanderhausen had settled in the southern Niagara Peninsula, where they had eventually acquired their own farms. There, on a farm located near the city of Kitchener, two young Banaters were getting married. All Alexanderhauseners living in and around Montreal were invited to the wedding. Since I had not yet acquired a car, I accepted Peter's invitation to attend this wedding along with him and his family. It was my first chance to experience the vastness of this huge country called Canada.

We left our homes early in the morning. Since Montreal is situated on a kind of island between two rivers, we had to cross a narrow two-lane bridge to reach the mainland. The bridge was blocked by a multitude of cars, so that the traffic almost came to a halt. This was my first experience with the phenomenon called traffic jam. Today there is an eight-lane highway crossing over an eight-lane bridge, but these were built a few years later.

According to the map, we had to cross a small corner of the province of Quebec to reach the province of Ontario. But the old highway ran through several towns and we reached Ontario later than we had expected. Here, only parts of the new, four—to six-lane highway had been completed. Time and again we had to revert back to the old highway, which run through a number of small towns, with their reduced speed limits. The distance between towns and villages was usually much greater than what we were used to in the Banat. We drove first along the St. Lawrence River to the town of Kingston, which is situated on Lake Ontario. It is the smallest of the five Great Lakes, but it stretches all the way from Kingston to Toronto. As we approached Toronto, we travelled already on the completed parts of highway number 401. The speed limit here was 60 miles per hour (slightly less than 100 km/h) and we made good progress. Even in the city, the highway had not yet reached its ultimate width of sixteen lanes. The traffic here was moderate and we did not even have to reduce our speed.

On this trip I saw very little of Toronto, which was then the second largest city of Canada.

We continued our drive on highway 401 in a south-westerly direction, through the southern-most part of Canada, with its fertile soil and mild climate. In the afternoon we reached the city of Kitchener. It is located a few miles north of the highway, so that we could not see much of it. We knew that the city was called Berlin before World War I and had been the unofficial capital of the Ontario-Germans.

We reached our destination late in the afternoon and there was a happy reunion of Alexanderhauseners belonging to at least three generations. It took place on the farm owned by my Uncle Nikolaus, or Nick, as we called him now. His wife and daughter had arrived from the Banat a few years before. Many of us were dead tired, but no one wanted to go to sleep, and we talked until deep into the night.

The wedding took place on the following day, with a beautiful ceremony in the church and a banquet in a large hall. On the way home, the distance appeared to be a little shorter, but it still took practically a day-long ride to get back to Montreal. Today, the completed highway has four or more lanes throughout, and the distance from Montreal to Toronto is 539 km. The trip would not take longer than five to six hours.

Little did I know at the time that during the decades that followed, my family and I would return many times to the Lukas farm. My aunt would always prepare authentic Banat-Swabian meals and Uncle Nick was well informed about issues of the past and present.


A few years later, I would get an even better impression of the huge expansion of Canada, when I went on a round trip by train from Montreal to the Pacific. The first half of the trip was by Canadian Pacific Railway and touched Ottawa, Toronto, Winnipeg (Manitoba), Regina (Saskatchewan), Calgary (Alberta) and through the Rocky Mountains to Vancouver (British Columbia or BC). The return trip was by Canadian National Railway and used in part a more northerly route, from Vancouver to Kamloops (BC), through the Rocky Mountains to Jasper (Alberta), Edmonton (Alberta), Saskatoon (Saskatchewan), then back to Winnipeg.

The first days stretched out in length. As the train sped westward, all one could see through the window was a rather monotonous landscape. Sometimes the train stopped at a small railway station, some people got on or off, some of them were native Indians. Only snow-white napkins and silver cutlery was used in the dining car. Passengers stayed there as long as they could, and talked to the people at their tables. In the evening, the conductors turned our seats into sleeping car berths. I climbed up into my upper berth, and slept like a baby. Nothing could disturb me, and the rattle of the wheels seemed perfect to promote falling asleep and sleeping through the night.

After a day and two nights I got off the train in Banff and was taken to the Banff Springs Hotel. This was an old and venerable luxury hotel operated by the Canadian Pacific Company. Dinner was served in a magnificent dining room with piano music. After dinner, a band played dance music. A highlight was the swimming pool filled with warm water from a natural hot spring.

The stay in Banff was followed by a beautiful train ride through the Rockies, as they call the Rocky Mountains here. The train had attached a few two-level observation cars, with tops of glass or clear plastic. There I sat drinking beer with two girls from England. We all marvelled at the sight of those beautiful mountains. Several peaks were over 11,500 feet (3500 meters) high and we were told that Mount Robson reached a height of 12,972 feet (3954 meters).

In Vancouver we stayed at the Hotel Vancouver. It was also operated by the Canadian Pacific Company, and was at the time the best hotel in the city. From the hotel I walked to the beach for my first swim in the Pacific Ocean. The location of the city, by the ocean and surrounded by mountains, was very impressive indeed. Nevertheless, the advertising claims that in Vancouver one could swim in the ocean and go skiing in the mountains on the same day, appeared just a touch exaggerated.

On our return trip we spent two days in Jasper, a spectacularly located resort in the Rocky Mountains. It sits in the valley of the Athabasca River and is connected in the east to Edmonton (Alberta) and in the west to Prince George (British Columbia) by the Yellowhead Highway and the Yellowhead Pass. The hotel was called Jasper Park Lodge and was a luxury hotel with individual bungalows scattered in the forest, and a beautiful restaurant in the main building. While the Banff Springs was an old-style luxury hotel, Jasper Park Lodge reflected luxury of a modern type.

After lunch I took a walk up the hill when I suddenly saw a black bear in front of me. The animal had not noticed me and was more preoccupied with the wild raspberries. I crept closer, while still staying behind the hedge, lifted my camera and squeezed the trigger. I could just see that the bear looked up, before I started my hasty retreat.

From Jasper we went back to Winnipeg and continued on to Montreal, once again taking a day and two nights to complete this portion of the trip. Now I had gained a better perspective of the immense size of this country. A glance at the map showed that my trip covered only part of the width of the country, from a province in the east to the Pacific. But I could barely imagine the massive land masses in the north. I knew only that many were not accessible by car or by train. Even ships could only reach some of them in summer, when the water was not frozen. Small aircraft could land there in the water during the summer and in the snow during the winter. The romantic sleighs pulled by Huskies were still in use there, but the natives were increasingly replacing them with snowmobiles.

# 29. Early travels

During my youth in the Banat I frequently felt trapped because I was prevented from visiting any country outside Romania. Even a visit to Hungary was virtually impossible at the time, and travel to the West was simply unthinkable. I could not even visit some of the villages surrounding Alexanderhausen, because the only means of transportation readily available were the railway and the bicycle. In many villages there were no places to stay overnight.

Now that I resided in Canada, I could travel anywhere I wanted, provided that I found the necessary time and money. It felt like a bird must have felt when it was released from its cage. It took me a couple of years to take root and get ready to travel outside of Canada. For that, I did not have to wait five years to become a citizen and obtain a passport. While I was still officially stateless, I could easily apply for a travel document. It looked very much like a passport, and was valid for travel anywhere in the world, but I needed a separate visa for each country that I wanted to visit.

From the American Consulate in Montreal I obtained a visitor visa, valid for four years, and it did not cost me a penny. During the following three years I made several trips to the USA. One of my first trips was to the city of New York. My strongest memory of that trip remains a flat tire during rush hours, on one of the elevated highways passing through the city. An endless stream of cars had to drive around me, while I mounted the spare wheel. I came away from it with some large scratches on both hands and a not exactly insignificant scare.

On a trip to Philadelphia I took several Montreal compatriots with me in my car. We visited some distant relatives and compatriots, including the relatives of the Beckers. I remember that they were a retired couple, not poor, but not rich either. When talk got around to the money I had left behind with the Beckers, they were surprised by the idea that the Beckers expected them to pay me its equivalent in dollars. They stated that they did not owe the Beckers anything, and had not even been consulted about such a deal. Now I knew that I could not count on my expected start-up money. The experience only confirmed the old adage that all beginnings are hard. I just had to earn my own money, like many immigrants before me and most likely after me.

In 1964 I took my first trip to Europe. I visited the Gilde family, with Hermann and Hilde. They had emigrated shortly after me and were living near the city of Ulm. Together we visited the Glass family in Bermatingen and the island of Mainau. A visit to my Schneider Uncle and aunt in Baden Baden included a beautiful hike through the Black Forest.

Then I visited the Beckers in the Hessian village that had become their new home. I could not bring myself to ask about the money that I had left behind with them. They were now two old people, making do with what they had and received from their state. I could not forget that they had been there for us when Oma and I passed through the hardest times of our lives. At the time of my visit, the difficult start was well behind me and my resources were adequate for my chosen lifestyle. Before returning to Canada I spent a few days in Vienna, visited Rome briefly, and admired some tourist attractions in Switzerland. The stays in each place were too short and I promised myself again and again, to return and stay for a longer time.

After five years of residence, I received the Canadian citizenship and with it the first real passport in my life. With it I visited Germany, Paris and London in 1967.

Three years later I went back to Germany, continued from there to Spain's Costa del Sol, with a side trip to Morocco. In those years, the Canadian dollar had a high exchange value when converted to many European currencies, so that the trips to Europe were quite affordable. I liked to visit relatives and friends who had already succeeded to emigrate from the Banat. During such visits, the conversations invariably turned to Alexanderhausen and to the Banat. I would have liked very much to extend my trips to the Banat, but the risk of such a journey still appeared irresponsibly high.

# 30. CONTINUING EDUCATION

Our offices were located in the city centre, in a seven-story building on Saint-Catherine Street West. The first floor was occupied by a branch of the Royal Bank, but our systems development group, with its several hundred engineers and technicians, occupied all the remaining floors. I had once again become a commuter. An electric commuter train running through a tunnel under Mount Royal brought me and hundreds of commuters from the Ahuntsic station to Central Station in about twenty minutes.

The function of my department was mainly the design of systems for the supply of energy to all types of telecommunications equipment, from telephone exchanges to cable carrier systems and microwave systems. It was ironic that my studies at the Polytechnic Institute of Temeswar had a power engineering focus, and I had actually studied the various aspects of telecommunications only during my service as a student in the Romanian army.

To give its young engineers a chance to become familiar with the various telecommunication systems that we supported, the company had set up a training department, which occupied the entire seventh floor. Gradually I completed almost all the offered courses. I found that it was important to know as much as possible about the telecommunication systems for which we designed the power delivery systems. All courses were presented by engineers, some of whom taught the same courses at McGill University. There were homework assignments and written examinations at the end of these courses.

My managers were always pleased when I did well in these tests. Our company participated in an advanced training course for engineers, sponsored by our parent company Bell Canada, and delivered at Queen's University in Kingston. The participants were selected on the basis of an application process. The company provided about fifty volunteers from our group with textbooks, primarily on higher mathematics and linear electric circuits, together with a plan of study. After studying these books on their own, all candidates had to write two exams. The candidates who obtained the best results at these exams were able to attend the courses at Queen's University. Attendance was entirely at the time and expense of the company.

I was one of four students selected from our group. We were invited to dinner in one of the top restaurants of the city, where our technical director congratulated us individually on our success. During one of the first autumn weeks, two of us went to Kingston and spent four weeks at Queen's University. After our return, the other two participants also spent four weeks at the university. This exchange was repeated throughout the entire semester. The first exams took place before the end of the year, with the final exams scheduled for June.

After the successful completion of the exams, we received our final diplomas, during a small ceremony with our professors. There were solemn speeches, and even alcoholic beverages were served, not commonplace in that environment at the time. The next day we said goodbye to each other and to Queen's University, and returned to our places of work.

After our return to Montreal our technical director invited all four of us to dinner at a restaurant on St. Helen's Island. This is an island in the St. Lawrence River, to the south of the larger island of Montreal. The restaurant was considered by many to be the best and most expensive in the city. Dinner started in the French manner with a dry sherry and finished with brandy and cigars. It gave each of us a taste of life in the upper bourgeois atmosphere that is seldom experienced by immigrants or even by ordinary Canadians. Since I was not a smoker, I took home the cigar in its own aluminum container. There it sat in a drawer of my desk for years, as a reminder of a pleasant evening and a really nice gesture on the part of the company, in recognition of our academic work.

In a personal letter, the course leader and Dean of the Faculty of Electrical Engineering stated among other things: ". . . I take this opportunity, on behalf of the University as well as myself, to commend you for a job supremely well done. The excellence of your work throughout the Course deserves special mention . . ." I knew that this was my last and best chance to continue my studies and to earn my doctorate. To do that, I would have to temporarily give up my job with the company and become a full-time student for a few years. When I discussed my options with my department head, he came up with an alternative proposal: He offered me a transfer to the new Department of Research and Development, which was being built jointly by the company and the parent company, in the city of Ottawa. After considering it for several days, I accepted the offer.

# 31. UNIVERSITIES

The old and venerable McGill University in Montreal was considered by many to be Canada's best university. It included a well-known faculty of engineering sciences, briefly called Engineering Department. After taking my first evening course at McGill, I was disappointed by the experience. The professor had simply not bothered to present the material in a coherent way, so that it could be mastered by us mature students. And our full-time jobs did not leave us enough time to acquire the course material on our own.

At Queen's University in Kingston the situation was very different. All the students in our group were adult engineers with several years of experience working for companies in the telecommunications industry. Our lectures were held in a building donated to the University by Bell Canada, and they were held exclusively for our group. It was the job of the professors to get us acquainted with the latest developments in electronics and telecommunications. As always, there were some professors who were better than others. A young assistant professor of Pakistani descent, who had only recently completed his doctorate in England, was teaching us the theoretical foundations of semiconductors. When about half of the students could not follow his lectures, they complained to the professor in charge of our course. They claimed that they could not understand what the instructor was saying. The assistant received a warning and had to start distributing facsimile course notes before each lecture.

Since we had to cover the course material for two months of regular courses in a single month, we had about twice as many lectures to attend as did regular students. On many days we had lectures both in the morning and in the afternoon. In addition to attending the lectures, we had to complete individual assignments which often required the use of the library or of the central computer of the University. We were fully occupied most of the time and had little free time.

Perhaps as compensation, our accommodation and food were exceptional. We lived in the residence for graduate students, where each one of us had a private room with bathroom. In every room there was a large desk with a modern table lamp and a telephone. We had unlimited use of the phone, courtesy of Bell Canada, but we also had to leave our phone number back at at our work places, so that we could be contacted in an emergency.

We had our breakfast and lunch with the regular students, in a cafeteria built in an old English style. Dinner was served to us in a private dining room of the graduate residence. No wine, beer or other alcoholic drinks were served for dinner, but a large billiard room was reserved for us. In it there was a large refrigerator and we kept it well stacked with beer. We also had at our disposal a large living room with several chairs and sofas, and a fairly large color TV. Night after night we watched the news on both the Canadian and American networks. We did not want to be completely cut off from the events of the world.

On a typical evening, each of us worked from about seven to eleven o'clock at his tasks, or tried to understand the course notes. Around eleven o'clock we usually met in the billiard room or living room for a short break. I usually drank a bottle of beer and went to sleep, while almost all the colleagues kept on working into the night.

During some weekends we had an opportunity to get acquainted with the city of Kingston. It is located on Lake Ontario and the Saint Lawrence River, and from 1841 to 1844 it was the first capital city of the united Canada. On the shore of the lake there were beautifully arranged paths. On mild spring days, it was inviting to walk there and think about God and the world.

The month spent at the University passed quickly each time, and then we had to return to our companies for another month of work. I remember that starting the car was not always easy, especially in the winter, after it had spent the whole month in the parking lot of the university. It was not a very long drive along highway 401 to Montreal. The colleagues coming from distant cities had to either use public transport, or even airplanes, to travel from Toronto to western Canada.

Our program at Queen's University also included the basics of the newly introduced electronic computers and their programming. It was obvious that these devices were destined to play an increasingly important role in the work of engineers. After my return to Montreal, I registered again at McGill University for four consecutive one-semester courses on computers, their programming and their applications in engineering. My move to Ottawa took place towards the end of these courses, but as I was commuting for some time between Montreal and Ottawa, I was able to successfully complete all four of these courses.

To solve one of the problems assigned to us during the first programming courses, we always started with a flowchart. From this we wrote a program in which each row was a statement of the program. The computer program thus consisted of several expressions similar to algebraic equations. We wrote these statements on so-called coding forms, which we handed to the staff of the computer room for the punching of the hole cards. Each line produced a punch card. After we had checked these cards, we brought them back to the computer room for processing by the computer. If they were absolutely correct, we received a computer-generated printout, with a listing of the program and the results it produced.

During subsequent courses we had to punch our own cards, in a perennially crowded room filled with punching machines. Other than that, the sequence of operations had not changed. Later on, in our laboratories in Ottawa, we did not need punch cards anymore because we were connected directly to the central computer by means of a teleprinter.

# 32. Old and new friendships

The school years in Temeswar and Alexanderhausen had naturally created friendships. We had traveled together over a significant distance along the path of life and had come to know each other. Sometimes someone had helped you; at other times you may have had a chance to help somebody else. Often we had experienced together a number of good or hard times, whether they lasted hours, days, weeks, or months.

When leaving the Banat, these friends were left behind. Some of them kept up their hopes that we would meet again some day, somewhere in the West. Most had to cope with life in the old country as best they could. It was best to celebrate one's departure as a happy event, which it was at least for the departing emigrant. With good company and a few bottles of wine, it could most often be made a joyous occasion, without any tears.

There were always the reciprocal promises to maintain the friendship by all possible means. We thought about visits, which at that time were possible only from the West to the East, and almost never in the opposite direction. We thought especially about maintaining our ties through correspondence. We promised to write each other, because it was easy and did not cost much money. We knew that phone calls were very expensive, if they were possible at all.

During my first years in Canada, I diligently wrote letters and to most of them I received answers. Soon, however, the intervals between the letters became longer. To some letters I never received an answer. It became increasingly clear that some letters never reached their destination. But one could never know whether a letter had been lost, or the recipient failed to respond for whatever reason.

Then I often waited until an occasion like Christmas or Easter came along. On these occasions I always sent many letters and cards. In some of these I mentioned in passing that I had not received an answer to a previous letter. That never helped to establish which letters had gone astray or which letters had never been written. That mystery could have been cleared up only by a personal conversation, and such conversations were just not in the cards. I did not contemplate travel to the Banat because of my fear of being held back there, and it would take many years before my friends would be able to travel to the West.

After decades, the political developments and the technological achievements actually lead to the resumption of many old friendships. An important role was played by the Internet, and especially by the wonderful invention of the e-mail. Not only were old friendships revived, but many new ones were created, some of which even led to mutual visits across the big pond.

Of my old classmates from Alexanderhausen, only Robert was living in Montreal. He and his mother were lucky to escape to Austria during the September days of 1944, when the battle front was in Alexanderhausen. From Austria they reached the American occupation zone of Germany, where no one tried to persuade them to repatriate to the Banat. When his father was released from the POW camp, he joined his family in a refugee camp. Daily life in the camp was hard, and there was a perennial shortage of food. As the prospects for the future were anything but rosy, the family took the first opportunity to immigrate to Canada.

In Montreal, the Kremling family lived like most of our compatriots who had chosen Canada as their new home. All family members worked and deposited their savings at the bank. When I arrived in Canada, the family was already living in a new bungalow located in one of the suburbs. In the beginning, Robert and I met quite often, to talk about our lost homeland, to play table tennis, and to drink a beer now and then. Just like Peter, Robert enjoyed hunting and fishing, as well as escaping to a hunting lodge located in the wilderness. Later on, our meetings became less frequent, and when Robert took a job in the oil fields of Alberta, they stopped almost completely.

Out of the many new acquaintances, very few resulted in real and enduring friendships. At work, at university, and through relatives and fellow countrymen one would meet many different people. Most of them belonged either to an older or to a younger generation. Their backgrounds and interests were often very different from one's own, although a few of the people met at work were of a similar age and had a somewhat similar background. It seemed, nevertheless, that the friendships formed at work rarely outlasted the time spent working together at the same company.

I had met my friend Harry at my first work place in Montreal. He had come to Canada from Yugoslavia about a year and a half earlier. As a technician, he probably earned even less than I did. I invited him to follow me to the second company, a move that certainly earned him a substantial salary increase. One day he appeared at the office with a beautiful and apparently quite expensive watch. He was very excited when he described to me how he had bought the watch. He had been walking down Saint-Catherine Street and had stopped in front of a shop window full of watches, just to admire the displayed products. The owner of the small watch shop came out, invited him into the store and asked him which watch he liked best. Harry pointed to a Swiss watch, but added that he did not have the kind of money to buy such a watch. Suddenly the dealer made him an entirely unexpected proposal:

"Pay as much as you can and then you can pay the rest in instalments."

Harry asked with surprise in his voice:

"How can you trust me, when you don't even know me?"

"I do not know you, but I can see that you are an honest man."

Harry was flattered and, after signing some papers, he stepped out onto Saint-Catherine Street again, wearing an expensive Swiss watch.

Harry learned from his experience that in Canada one could buy many things on credit. A week later he arrived at work in a huge Pontiac convertible, a true street cruiser. The car was not exactly new, but still cost a lot of money. It was to be paid in monthly instalments, over a three year period. If Harry would miss any of these monthly payments, the car would be repossessed by the dealer. But Harry did not worry about that:

"Even if I lose the car in the end, the time I was able to drive around in it was great fun."

Harry left that company before me, and I never found out if he paid all the money he owed on the car, to finally become its real owner. It took me a while longer to realize that most Canadians bought many things in instalments, from appliances to furniture and cars. Purchase on credit was not for me, since the interest paid on these loans seemed to be a waste of money. As a born and raised Banat Swabian, I was used to save the money first, before spending it.

# 33. ENCOUNTERS AND ACQUAINTANCES

During the two years following my graduation from the Polytechnic Institute, many friends and schoolmates from Temeswar and Alexanderhausen had been getting married. Concentrating on my objective of emigration, I maintained my self-imposed imperative: Marriage remained out of the question for me, as I was determined to stick to my agenda at all costs. How long one could maintain a friendship with a girl, without it leading to marriage, was a question that every individual had to answer for himself.

I found not only the girls in the New World to be different, but also the interpersonal relationships. It seemed to me that, while most girls in the Banat had been single and unattached, Canadian girls seemed to have had boyfriends starting in grade school. In Temeswar one could invite a girl to a movie, a concert or a sporting event, and meet her at an agreed-upon meeting place in the city. Canadian girls expected to be picked up by car at their home, which also offered a good opportunity to meet their parents. Getting to know the parents at this time seemed premature to me: It looked too much like a firm commitment, such as an engagement or even a marriage. It appeared logical to me, that before such a commitment, people needed more time to get to know each other. For those born and raised in Canada, common schooling and social activities may have provided that time. An immigrant in his mid-twenties would miss most of these chances for socialisation.

One thing that kept me at home in my room quite often, were the books. Suddenly I had access to a great variety of wonderful books. All the books I wanted to read earlier in my life, but could not get, were now available and even affordable. From a book club in Germany I could order beautiful leather-bound volumes, from Goethe to Thomas Mann, and from Hermann Hesse to Robert Lenz. Then there were the philosophers from Leibniz to Hegel and from Schopenhauer to Nietzsche. A strong Canadian dollar, worth four German Marks, made the books quite inexpensive. I ordered to my heart's content, and soon accumulated a considerable number of books in my improvised bookcase.

I spent many evenings and weekends reading, but on some Saturday nights I took my car to the city centre and went to the movies. I hardly ever visited a bar alone, but preferred to try them out in the company of colleagues. We found that the noise usually made any meaningful conversation quite impossible. In some bars, customers were encouraged to buy cheap wine for the naked girls under the pretext that it was champagne. Touching the "actresses" was strictly forbidden. They were probably reserved for the bar owners and for the various bosses of the underworld.

I remember a Saturday evening when I went with two colleagues to an upscale bar located in downtown Montreal. We ended up inviting three French-Canadian girls to join us at our table. We had all brought our cars, so each one of us was able to drive one of the ladies to her home. On Sunday afternoon we boys met to share our experiences. None of us had been invited into a home, as each of the three girls claimed to live either with parents or relatives. Each of us had obtained a phone number, but we felt somehow disappointed and decided scrap these numbers.

I met some girls who had come from Germany and did not have a Danube-Swabian background. Unfortunately, the few girls I met appeared to be superficial, insincere and untrustworthy. In my native Banat we would have said that they were more conceited than educated. As an example, I remember Gerda, a girl I met through family connections. She eventually married a man also born in Germany. At their wedding, the man's best friend served as best man. Several years and two children later, the wife of the best friend died suddenly. Soon after, the neighbours noticed that Gerda was meeting the new widower in a neighbouring motel. One day she was confronted at the motel by her husband. That did not faze her at all. She told him calmly that she now loved his best friend, and that he could have the children. Soon after that incident, she left the city with the new lover. The affair reminded me of a quick prayer heard in the Banat: "Of such calamity, may God preserve us!"

A few Danube-Swabian families living in Montreal had daughters of an age close to mine. Most of these girls were either married or had boyfriends. The younger ones were either born in Canada or at least had grown up here. They had become true North American girls and would only be impressed by expensive sports cars and possibly by some performers of popular songs and dances. I could not relate to these things, either because I did not grow up with them, or because I was simply too old to take them seriously.

At a summer festival of the German community of Montreal that took place on the plateau in front of the so-called Chateau Mont Royal, I met Elizabeth, the daughter of a family originating from the Banat. Her parents had been born in Canada and had become rich during the war and postwar period. I had barely exchanged a few words with her in passing, but I really liked the girl. Some months later, after a few glasses of wine and some encouragement by others, I found the courage to call her. She remembered the summer festival, but unfortunately did not remember me. And she obviously did not want to meet this unknown guy speaking with a vaguely middle-European accent. I found out that Elizabeth attended Sunday mass at the St. Boniface Catholic Church, but rarely took part in Danube-Swabian or other German entertainment. Since I did not regularly attend these events either, a chance encounter simply did not come about.

I still remembered the girl during my stay at Queen's University in Kingston, so I wrote her a letter from there. When I received no answer, I finally recognized the futility of my efforts. The fact that her family was rich obviously proved an insurmountable obstacle to the establishment of any kind of relationship. To some people, possibly including the girl and her parents, it made me look like somebody who wanted to marry for money. Those who knew me better were certain that this was absolutely not the case. But the girl did not know me and did not want to get to know me. The situation reminded me of a sentence that I had read somewhere: Of all the money earned in life, the part earned by marriage is by far the hardest earned. I decided to keep this sentence in mind and accept things the way the way they had developed.

Many years later I learned by accident that Elizabeth's grandmother had insisted from the beginning that her granddaughter should marry only a medical doctor. Most doctors in Canada were indeed making a lot of money, but was an excess of money really a necessary and sufficient condition for a happy life? Decades later I learned, again by accident, that Elizabeth had never married and lived alone in Toronto.

# 34. WORLD'S FAIR IN MONTREAL

I will always retain fond memories of the summer of 1967. At that time, the world's fair called Expo 67 took place in Montreal, on an island partially reclaimed from the St. Lawrence River. It is almost impossible to believe today, that 62 countries, all Canadian provinces and many cities did not shy away from the costs to show their best side to the world. The various pavilions and their interiors, the salaried staff, the food and drinks, all cost a lot of money. We, the visitors, had to pay our entrance fees and the costs of food and drink, but none of us seemed to have any doubts that it was all affordable and worthwhile.

Expo 67 was one of the most successful exhibitions in the world and for many Canadians it will always be associated with a dose of nostalgia. For some, it was one of the biggest events of the 20th Century. In Canada, the year 1967 is often described as the last good year before the beginning of economic decline, the expressed desire of many Quebecers to secede from Canada, and the widespread political apathy gripping the country.

I purchased a universal pass, which gave me access to all public pavilions, although some pavilions and several restaurants charged an additional entrance fee. In front of many pavilions the queues seemed permanent, and the restaurants of many nations were almost always full of people. In front of many pavilions, and in additional spaces provided for the purpose, the artistic and cultural presentations of various kinds never seemed to stop. In front of the pavilion of the Federal Republic of Germany, a brass band from Germany was often playing, and in front of the Mexican Pavilion one could listen to the mariachis regularly flown in from Mexico.

In the evening the pavilion restaurants were even more crowded than during the day. A short walk led to the entertainment centre of the island where there were a number of great restaurants. Probably the largest and most successful of these restaurants was the German beer garden. English and French Canadians, as well as visitors from around the world, knew at least one German word: Biergarten. There, the beer was good and the music was loud, people were swaying and after midnight even dancing on the tables. On a yellowed photograph I can see even today how the members of my entire department were enjoying themselves. It is amazing how young we were!

During the days of Expo'67 cultural organizations from several countries presented programs in Montréal. An international opera series was presented in the great hall of the cultural centre named Place des Arts. I managed to get tickets for all performances in this series. The opera "Faust" by Charles Gounod was presented by the Montreal Symphony Orchestra / L'Orchestre Symphonique de Montréal; "Tristan and Isolde" by Richard Wagner and "A Masked Ball by Giuseppe Verdi were both presented by the Stockholm Royal Opera; and the operas "The Marriage of Figaro" by Wolfgang Amadeus Mozart and "Wozzeck" by Alban Berg were both presented by the Vienna State Opera. All in all, it was a unique experience. The series revived my passion for this art form, born in my student days in Temeswar, and badly neglected during the previous years in Montreal.

The new underground public transportation system, officially called Le Metro, was now in full operation and made a stop at the Expo site. I found it most convenient to park my car near a metro station in the west of Montreal and take the metro to the Expo site. The return trip, usually late at night, was also a good chance to diminish the effects of a few glasses of beer enjoyed during the evening. I spent many a summer evening on the Expo grounds, both during the week and on weekends.

It was the last evening of the Expo, when I was sitting with a group of boys and girls in a restaurant near the Mexican pavilion. We drank beer and listened to the music of the mariachis. I started talking to a girl sitting next to me at the large table. The conversation became more and more interesting. Soon the girl had my full attention, and I hardly noticed that the other people at our table were fading into the background. She was a laboratory technician in a hospital in the city, her name was Donna, and I promised to call her.

# 35. THE LATE SIXTIES

During the following weeks and months, I frequently met Donna. At first we just went to a cinema on Saturday night, then we added the occasional dinner in a restaurant, and later some car rides on Sunday, in the countryside surrounding the city. On a beautiful fall weekend we went to the picturesque old Quebec City. Eventually we extended these trips to the nearby states of New York, Vermont, New Hampshire and Maine.

These were the times of long hair and long sideburns, of the discotheques and the hippies. For a while we found the incredibly high noise levels in discos to be quite exciting. Later on we were annoyed by the drinks, which were expensive and of poor quality. Soon our interest turned to the better restaurants, and to the so-called supper-clubs, which offered dinner and dancing.

I remember a New Year's Eve in a restaurant located on the top floor of the Ville-Marie skyscraper. A delicious dinner was served very slowly, so that it lasted until midnight, when they served champagne for a toast to the New Year. Throughout the night, a good orchestra played for dancing and listening. Today we would describe it as an entertainment form of the so-called good old days. It was very popular at that time among people who could afford it.

The younger generation, or at least a good part of it, followed the hippie philosophy: "Don't trust anybody over thirty". According to our ages, Donna and I were situated in the no man's land between the so-called "generation of baby boomers" and the more traditionally oriented older generation. The baby boomers were the large number of children born right after the Second World War, and we were both a little older than that. We did not share the claim of the hippies, that they could not trust their parents. The fact that they saw their parents as overworked materialists seemed unconscionable to us. It was, after all, the work of the parents that had made their carefree lives possible. The use of drugs appeared to us as a shortsighted and irresponsible habit, which we would never adopt.

But no one could deny that we lived in an uncertain world. Many people of that time seemed to have given up their faith in the future. The Cuban missile crisis of 1962 had brought the world close to its self-destruction. The Soviet Union seemed to spare no effort and leave no stone unturned in its quest for world domination. The most desirable option for the Soviets would have been to reach their goal through the so called "peace movement" that they supported and funded. But they seemed prepared to use nuclear weapons, if necessary to achieve their goal.

The danger in which the world found itself was illustrated by the so called Doomsday Clock. Since 1947 its dial was kept up-to-date by the Board of the Bulletin of Atomic Scientists at the University of Chicago. The updates were based on the international situation and the important events happening in the world. The more the displayed time approached midnight, the closer the world appeared to its final demise. Whenever a new country came into the possession of nuclear weapons, the big hand was moved closer to midnight; when there were signs of disarmament or relaxation of international relations, the big hand was moved back from midnight.

In the 1960s, this clock usually indicated seven to ten minutes before midnight. These "minutes to the end", while not strictly scientific, but rather empirically determined, certainly helped to underline the apocalyptic mood of a significant proportion of youth in North America and elsewhere in the world.

The feeling of pending doom and lack of confidence in a secure future was pretext enough for the hippies and for many others, to embark on an intense and often reckless life, or to live from one day to the next. Everyone wanted to enjoy as much as possible today, because the future was a big question mark. At some point I asked myself whether it was justifiable to start a family under these circumstances, and to bring children into this kind of a world.

We rarely talked about it, but I knew that Donna was often worried about us and our common or separate future. She understood the uncertainty of our world, but she did not believe that we should let this instability define our lives.

This theme became acute when my transfer to Ottawa was imminent. I pointed out that only a two-hour trip by train, bus or car separated the cities of Ottawa and Montreal. Donna was afraid that my transfer could lead to the end of our long relationship. After a few tears were shed, we agreed to a temporary break in our relationship. I would be very busy for a while, looking for accommodation, arranging the move to Ottawa, and getting aquainted with my new job. Donna was kept busy by her own work in Montreal. We agreed to use this time to think about whether and how we should continue.

# 36. IN THE CAPITAL CITY

All I knew about the Canadian capital city of Ottawa, I had learned on a one-day visit, which had taken place several years before my transfer. On a beautiful Sunday morning, Robert and I had traveled by car from Montreal to Ottawa. We admired the Parliament buildings and their associated outbuildings, drove around in the city, and stopped at some beautiful parks. At noon we started looking for a restaurant. Finding a restaurant was not easy, because many restaurants were closed on Sunday. When we finally found a restaurant that was open, we were unable to order a beer, because no beer was served on a Sunday in the Province of Ontario.

In recent years, the city had grown larger and much in it had changed for the better. In the city centre, several high-rises had been built. None of these were located in the immediate vicinity of the Parliament buildings, as they were not allowed to overshadow Parliament. The offices and laboratories of my company were located west of the city, inside the official Green Zone.

I looked at several apartments in the west end of the city, but was not impressed by any of them. Just five minutes east of my place of work, in the Bayshore neighbourhood, a new eleven-storey building was nearing completion. It contained condominium apartments, some of which were still available for purchase. I liked what I saw and signed the purchase contract for a one-bedroom apartment with a large balcony. It was located on the tenth floor and was equipped with shiny new kitchen appliances. I agreed to a suitable move-in date, subject to approval of an acceptable mortgage by my bank.

My new department manager allowed generous time for my apartment purchase and move. I had to deal not only with the construction company, but also with lawyers, bank officials and furniture suppliers. The movers packed my belongings in Montreal and brought them to Ottawa with only minor damages. The apartment had built-in connections for telephone and cable TV. I connected the phone immediately, but as yet owned no TV and did not miss it either.

It was on a on a Sunday, two or three weeks after my move to Ottawa, when I sat in my nice little apartment and suddenly felt very lonely. My department manager had invited me to dinner once, but it occurred to me that besides him, I did not know anybody in this strange city. I picked up the phone and dialled Donna's number in Montreal. She seemed glad to hear my voice, and I invited her to visit me on the next weekend.

On the following Friday evening I awaited Donna at the bus terminal and took her to the new apartment for a homemade dinner. It was followed by two beautiful autumn days during which we visited the capital city and its surrounding area. When I took Donna back to the bus terminal early on Monday morning, I asked her if she would like to move to Ottawa. She said she would think about it.

When I called her later in the week, Donna immediately asked if I was serious when invited her to move into my small apartment. I was expecting the question and said yes without hesitation. After a few seconds silence, she finally said:

"I think I just heard a marriage proposal, and as you know only too well, that makes me a very happy person. When should I move?"

"First you have to resign from your work and find a moving company. I hope to be able soon to spread out the welcome mat."

As autumn came to an end, we were together, and felt very cosy in our small but nice apartment. Donna had brought some pieces of furniture that complemented my own. After the holidays she took a job in a hospital. The new job was not as good as her previous job in Montreal, but it was nevertheless a start, because she did not want to sit at home. When we passed a jewellery store in the city centre, I asked Donna to select a beautiful ring for herself. That sealed our pact and made it clear to everybody, that we were now properly engaged.

It was not important for us to share the news with the rest of the world. Even my father and the rest of the family in Montreal knew nothing about it. I was pretty sure that they suspected something, but the relationship between us had cooled considerably after my move to Ottawa. For the time being, we did not think about any mutual visits.

By this time, living together without formal marriage was no longer a rarity. The hippies were living together in communes, and in the province of Quebec, neither the church nor the civil marriage was a prerequisite for living together and bringing up children. This form of cohabitation would soon find recognition in the laws of many countries.

# 37. A family of my own

My new job required a return to the fundamentals of electrical engineering and in particular of telecommunications. In our laboratories, the latest instruments were readily available, including very high performance oscilloscopes the likes of which I had not seen before. These were the years during which the semiconductor technology made unprecedented strides forward. The capability and versatility of semiconductor components was forever expanding and we were often the first users of the newly developed components. We had direct access to the inventors of the new devices, either in person or by telephone. We even had a department that did basic research on the physics of semiconductors and the newly developed devices. We could always discuss the properties and behaviour of these new devices with our in-house engineers and scientific staff.

Our work had to take into account the needs of our parent company Bell Canada. It was in the process of modernizing its central offices and other telecommunication systems. We solved problems of compatibility between old and new equipment and dealt with issues that had previously never received the attention they deserved. We established the cost and schedule for the individual segments of each project together with colleagues from Bell Canada, and were then free to choose the best approaches for the timely completion of the work.

It was demanding work and it gave us much satisfaction. For the first time in my career I felt that I was able to apply in my daily work what I had learned at university, while also keeping up with ongoing technological developments. This was indeed the type of work that I wanted and felt that I deserved in the old country, but could never have obtained under the political constraints of the time.

Since Donna worked as well, we shared the household tasks, and they were far from onerous. She usually took the bus in the morning, but often I would pick her up by car in the afternoon. On the weekends we often visited the beautiful lakes and meadows located close to Ottawa, along the

Quebec side of the Ottawa River, or Algonquin Park with its many lakes. Sometimes we would even drive to the Laurentian hills, as we had done before, when we lived in Montreal.

It was on a Christmas Day, when we were sitting on the sofa, completely relaxed, with a bottle of wine on the little table in front of us. The little Christmas tree was full of lights, and a fine pine scent was emanating from it. On television, a Christmas story for children was being shown. One of us asked the question: Wouldn't it be nice to have a complete family, with a child or two running around? We agreed to let nature take its course.

I had no doubt that our decision would soon have consequences. Ironically, some second thoughts came into my mind at work: the child should have a name, and being married would help ensure that it did. In the evening, I explained my plan to Donna: We had been talking about a week's holiday in the south and that was a good opportunity for getting married. Donna mentioned that she would likely loose her job in the process, but we agreed that such a possibility would not hold us back.

The same Ottawa jeweller, who had produced our engagement rings, was only too happy to supply two wedding rings of the same sizes. Then I booked a holiday week for two in Miami, Florida. We were formally and officially married at the local registry office. Afterwards, when we strolled down the beautiful tropical Lincoln Boulevard, I handed my camera to a young man who happened to pass by, and asked him to take some pictures of us.

We chose one of these photos as our wedding picture. When I look at it today, I am transported back to the early seventies of the twentieth century. Donna is wearing a long dress with blue flowers on a white background; I am wearing an almost white jacket with barely perceptible light blue stripes. Donna is wearing sunglasses, large but not very dark. I have a two-tone pink tie around my neck; and I have long hair and long sideburns. Yes, that is the way we were, and that is how the times were.

After an excellent seafood dinner with a great bottle of white wine, on the way to our hotel, we passed a post office. Donna suddenly decided to send a telegram to her parents living in western Canada, to briefly inform them about the events of the day. As she prepared her telegram, I prepared a similar telegram for my father in Montreal: "Just married. Arriving Wednesday 14:30 o'clock in Dorval. Donna and your son." I knew that our airplane tickets provided for a change of planes in Montreal. If anybody wanted to await us in Dorval, or even pick us up for a coffee, we would simply interrupt our trip in Montreal, and continue to Ottawa later. Donna was not convinced that my telegram was a good idea, but I sent it off anyway. It was no surprise to us, that on the day we returned, nobody awaited us at the Dorval airport.

We changed planes in Montreal in accordance with our tickets, and arrived back home in our cozy little apartment by evening. We had done what we thought was right and the Montrealers had acted according to their own knowledge and belief.

Donna and I continued our work and the time passed quickly. After several reminders from Donna, I called Montreal and spoke with my father and with Anna. I did not ask whether they had received the telegram sent from Miami, or whether they could not decide on a response. It was unimportant to us and we never mentioned the matter again. We made several visits to Montreal, and relations improved rapidly, especially after our announcement that Donna was expecting a child. I insisted that she give up her job and devote herself fully to her new role.

Now we had to rearrange our lives around other priorities. We concluded that our apartment was too small for a family of three. We needed a children's room and a backyard or garden, where a child could play outdoors. The time had come for us to start looking for a house. After much searching we found a small bungalow located a short distance from my place of work. The asking price was only about 5000 dollars more than what I had planned to pay.

Our new home had three bedrooms, a living room combined with a dining room, a kitchen and a bathroom. The basement was unfinished, except for a small room with an already installed washing machine and electric dryer. Under the same roof as the house was a garage, just big enough for one car and some tools and utensils. The paved driveway was long enough to park at least two other cars.

In June we moved into our new home and in October our son Raimund came into this world. I will never forget my excitement when I was walking up and down a long corridor at the Ottawa Civic Hospital, while Donna had to come to grips with the infinitely more difficult tasks in the delivery room. Time passed slowly, the wait seemed to have no end. Finally a nurse came out and announced: "It's a boy, mother and baby are doing well."

A miracle had happened. A perfect little human being had been born, according to the eternal laws that need not necessarily be understood before believing in them. When compared to this miracle, the daily events and frequent catastrophes in the world seemed trivial and of little importance. Throughout their long history, the inhabitants of the earth had often believed that the apocalypse was imminent. But the world had survived all the real and imaginary disasters and the miracle I had just experienced renewed my hope that the earth would somehow survive even our nuclear age.

We brought the little bundle of life home and laid it in the crib in the newly spruced up nursery. When we watched the baby sleeping peacefully in his crib, the world seemed full of hope and expectation, full of unlimited possibilities. Like so many parents all over the world, we were determined to do everything possible to support the new life with all our strength and to shelter it from all dangers.

What followed were months of interrupted sleep, diapers hung all over the house, many scheduled doctor appointments for mother and child. Most of the time, I was able to take Donna and the child by car to wherever they needed to go. When that was not possible, often a neighbour lady with a car would help. Only in rare cases was a taxi needed. It was a very busy time in our lives. We instinctively understood its importance, but only later could we fully appreciate its beauty.

Before Raimund was two years old, we took him on a trip to the province of Saskatchewan, as it was high time that I met Donna's parents. They had retired and lived in the city of Regina. Their parents had arrived from Russia around the turn of the century. I remember a picnic in a park, where we grilled sausages and patties, and drank copious amounts of German wine. We travelled by car to visit Donna's sister on a farm near Yorkton. One evening we were all sitting outside as the night descended. We watched a lighted object moving silently across the sky, and we were not sure whether it was a satellite or an UFO. When the sky went dark, it suddenly lit up in a profusion of colours. I had never witnessed the aurora borealis before that night.

In May 1974 we received a call from Anna in Montreal, telling us that my father had suffered a heart attack and was in the hospital. I immediately drove to Montreal and two hours later stood in front of his hospital bed. My father was connected to various tubes and wires, and he spoke very slowly. Anna went out into the corridor to leave us alone for a few minutes. Unfortunately, we did not have much to say to each other. I had missed him during the seventeen years while I was growing up, but he had missed my mother even more during his last thirty years. I did not want to mention what we both had lost, and I could not talk about death and dying at all. When I had to leave, I could say nothing better than:

"Just keep up the good fight; you will be all right again."

"My good fight is over and so is my life. Your mother had to die at a much younger age."

Those turned out to be his last words to me. At the funeral, Donna and I were riding with Anna in a very big black car, first to St. Boniface Church, and then to the Côte-des-Neiges Cemetery. After the service Ann invited us to dinner, together with other close relatives. I grieved for my father; he had lived through a hard life and died at the age of only 66 years.

Anna gave me a copy of my father's last will and mentioned that she had signed an identical document. According to these testaments, all property was left to the surviving spouse. On the death of the surviving spouse, the property was to be divided into two equal parts, one of which to be given to me and the other to Ann. That seemed eminently reasonable to me, and I paid no further attention to the matter.

My father - Titus Tullius, 1953

As an only child myself, I would have been happy with a single child, but Donna did not abandon her belief that Raimund should have a brother or sister. After almost two and a half years, our second son, Konrad, was born. Again I was walking up and down a long corridor at the Ottawa Civic Hospital, while Donna again did the infinitely harder work in the delivery room. Once again, time seemed to stand still and the wait seemed endless. And once again a nurse came out and announced: "It's a boy; mother and baby are doing well."

Now Raimund had to move into one of the two larger bedrooms and Konrad was given the nursery with all its decorations. Donna and I were already used to the interrupted sleep, and the diapers were now made entirely of paper, to be thrown away after use. Even the doctor appointments for mother and child seemed to be easier and less stressful. We had settled in and believed that we had reached a steady-state condition.

It came as a surprise, when some managers of the company wanted me to lead a small development team in Montreal. Since I could not refuse the invitation out of hand, I went to Montreal to meet the members of my prospective department. I knew about half of them from my days in Montreal, and one of them had actually been my boss some years before. The people seemed to expect me, and that made a rejection even more difficult. During dinner in a very chic restaurant, a vice president of the company did his best to convince me that all the conditions for the success of this department were in place, only my acceptance was missing.

After exhaustive discussions with Donna, we decided to accept the offer. We found a house in the city section of Ville Mont-Royal and moved there. I had just connected our TV set to its cable, when the newscaster announced the result of the provincial elections. To our great surprise, the Parti Quebecois turned out to be the winner of these elections. The program of this party was to take the province of Quebec out of the Canadian confederation. This result was bad news for the economy and in a few days the price of our newly purchased home fell by about one third.

At my workplace, I soon found out that the circumstances were not exactly as they had previously presented them to me. My opinion, so highly praised before my acceptance of the position, now counted for little and was regularly ignored. I was supposed to only support the preconceptions of others and to implement concepts that I judged to be faulty.

An even more important fact was that the language laws and rules adopted by the Government of the Province of Quebec allowed our children to attend only French schools. As a member of a national minority during my earlier life in the Banat, I had an innate understanding for the efforts of French-speaking Canadians, to preserve their language and culture. But the obvious efforts of the Provincial Government to turn the children of immigrants into French-speaking Québécois reminded me too much of the attempts that the former Hungarian authorities had made to make Magyar-speaking Hungarians out of my German-speaking ancestors. I felt strongly that in a free country such as Canada, the selection of schools belonged to us, the parents. With each passing day, we became more convinced that the prospects for a future without an overbearing government were better in Ottawa than in the Province of Quebec.

# 38.  BACK IN OTTAWA

The transfers of personnel between various company locations were usually intended for a period of two years. As our second year in Montreal drew to a close, I focussed on the planning of our return to Ottawa. It was easy to give up the post of department head and return to the research and development work. When the department in Montreal had to give up its utopian plans and get back to concentrate on routine work, my family moved back to Ottawa. House prices in Montreal had already recovered and my department in Ottawa paid not only for the move, but also compensated us for the small loss resulting from the purchase and sale of our Montreal home.

In the west of Ottawa, the new suburb called Kanata was developing rapidly. We found some houses under construction on a quiet crescent, one of which seemed to be ideally suited for our small family. The important thing was that to get to my work from there took only a car ride of about ten minutes. On the top floor of our new house there were four spacious bedrooms and a bathroom. On the ground floor, there was the entrance hall, a guest toilet, living room, family room, dining room and a spacious kitchen. The basement was not completely finished, but it contained the furnace of the new central heating, as well as connections for a washing machine and for an electric dryer.

In the fall we moved back to Ottawa, just in time to enrol Raimund for his kindergarten classes. Donna did not take on another job; she just wanted to be a full-time mother, and I thought that it was a great idea. I went back to the work that I had given up two years earlier. In the meantime the company had grown and expanded into several leased buildings. When our department moved into one of these buildings, my daily commute to work increased to between 20 and 30 minutes, which was still significantly less than my daily drive to work had been in Montreal.

The digital switching system developed in our labs and manufactured by Telecom-owned factories was a great success at home and abroad. It was the first of its kind in the world and it proved to be reliable and cost-effective. It had its biggest sales success in the U.S., where the famous Bell Labs took two additional years to introduce a similar system. Telecom established a subsidiary in the U.S., in the state of North Carolina. The place was called Research Triangle Park and was located between the cities of Raleigh and Durham. Large production facilities were built, and the laboratories and offices of our research and development organization were erected across the road from the factory.

Like many colleagues, I was asked if I wanted to transfer to the new labs in North Carolina, where engineers with relevant experience were urgently needed. The company invited me and my family to take a trip to North Carolina, so that we could evaluate the local living and working conditions ourselves. As it was the middle of summer, this was a good opportunity to make the trip by car and take the whole family along. It was a two-day drive to our hotel in Research Triangle Park.

We spent three days there, during which we visited Raleigh, Durham and the surrounding area. We looked at public buildings, such as libraries and hospitals, as well as at grocery stores and department stores. We visited a colleague who had moved to the area a year or two before. He was proud of his swimming pool in the backyard of his own home, in which he swam a few laps on most days of the year. He spent very little money on heating, but had to use electric air conditioning through much of the year. The South was obviously quite different from our northern city of Ottawa. Since I had two weeks of vacation ahead of me, we continued our drive to Myrtle Beach, a beach resort on the Atlantic coast, in the state of South Carolina. The water was wonderfully warm and our two boys were fascinated by the waves. The beach, with its white sand, was exceptionally wide and seemed to be endless.

But even before we started the journey home, Donna and I had decided to stay in Ottawa. The people in the South and their behaviour seemed somehow different from what we knew from Ottawa and Montreal. We were used to the people and the environment of Ottawa; we had been living there for awhile and felt at home there. Our boys were doing very well in the Canadian school system. They were both in so-called "enriched classes" and each had skipped a grade. We wanted to focus our efforts on them; we wanted it to be their time, not ours. A switch to a different school system seemed a little risky. And we all loved the changing of the seasons and particularly the renewal of nature after its long winter sleep.

Once we settled down in our Kanata home, our lives returned quickly to the pattern we had established before the temporary move to Montreal. Both of our boys attended English schools in which about half of the subjects of study were taught in French. This French immersion was intended to produce bilingual students, that is, students able to work in both official languages of the country. In most cases, the program did not succeed completely, because nobody could prevent the children from speaking English during breaks and at home, or ensure ongoing preoccupation with the second language after graduation.

Early on I tried to speak German at home, with Raimund and with Donna, who was at the time taking German lessons at the Goethe Institut in Ottawa. Unfortunately, the English-speaking world surrounding us, all the neighbours, neighbourhood kids, books, newspapers, magazines, radio and television made these efforts very difficult. We registered our boys with the German Saturday School, where they spent at least one day a week in a German environment. They were exposed not only to reading and writing, but also to songs and fairy tales, a bit of drama and poetry in German. The Christmas celebrations, summer picnics and graduation parties for children and parents were always memorable experiences.

Even after the death of my father we visited Anna, Ann, and Mr. Demeter in Montreal, and they visited us in Ottawa, especially during the good-weather seasons. Anna always came across as the good-natured grandmother, giving generous gifts of money to our young boys. When Ann called and told us that her mother was in the hospital, we first did not assume anything bad. When Ann made an urgent appeal to me to visit her mother for probably the last time, I drove to Montreal. Anna was in the same hospital where I had seen my father for the last time. She could not speak, and I did not know if still recognized me. Anna seemed to suffer from attacks of fear. It was impossible to determine whether it was just fear of dying or fear of the encounter with her creator.

Donna and I drove to Montreal for the funeral, which was similar to the funeral of my father, all the way to the grave in the Côte-des-Neiges cemetery. After the funeral, we drove back to Ottawa, because we were not invited to the dinner Ann had arranged for the relatives from her side of the family. Several days later she told us on the phone that she would open the testament of her mother only after six weeks had passed. When some ten weeks passed and nothing happened, I called her and asked her about it. She suggested that I should meet with Mr. Demeter, who would give me all the necessary explanations.

The meeting took place in the restaurant of a small town located midway between Ottawa and Montreal. From Mr. Demeter I learned that Anna had changed her last will after the death of my father. This time no relatives or countrymen had signed as witnesses; there were only some unknown French names. It became clear, and I confirmed it later, that the changes had been made very quietly, so that no relatives or compatriots knew anything about them. In the new version of her testament Anna had transferred all her assets to her daughter Ann. In addition, Mr. Demeter informed me, all the homes that had previously been jointly owned by the two families, had been transferred to Ann as their sole owner. He handed me a copy of the will and our meeting ended without as much as a goodby.

Thus the relationship between my family and this second family of my father died of a natural death. It was not about a bunch of corn stalks, as it once supposedly had happened in Alexanderhausen between two brothers. Here they had deprived me and my family of our fair share of my father's estate. As Peter Schwarz later assured me, my father had received a considerable sum of money from Germany, as compensation for what he had lost in the Banat. It was with this money, that the two families purchased their first rental property. How much my fair share was could have been discussed and agreed upon, among people of good will. But Ann and Mr. Demeter were concerned only about accumulating property at all costs. Now they had feathered their nest and that was all that mattered to them.

# 39. VISITING THE BANAT AGAIN

After several years of planning, a process in which the whole family participated, we were all ready to take an extended trip to Europe. Donna and the children were looking forward to this trip and I was eager to get them to meet relatives in Germany, Austria and Hungary. In addition, we unanimously decided to extend our trip to the Banat.

It was the year 1985, and after an absence of nearly 25 years, I believed the time had come at last to show my family my birthplace and my native region, the Banat. Our boys were then 12 and 9 years old and were eager to see Europe. I discussed the trip with the security officers of our company, and they concluded that the risk was acceptable, as long as I kept myself out of the well-known situations usable for extortion. As Canada reacted strongly to any unfair treatment of its citizens abroad, proper treatment by the Romanian authorities could be expected.

At Frankfurt airport we stepped into a rental car and drove to Rastatt. Uncle Johann and his wife, my aunt, now lived there, together with cousin Hans and his wife. They had managed to emigrate a few years earlier, after our common grandmother had died in 1968. Cousin Kathi had sold the house in Alexanderhausen and had moved to Temeswar with her husband. We spent a few hectic days in Rastatt. On Sunday, many Alexanderhauseners now living in Rastatt and its surroundings came to visit. Seeing them again was a great joy and called for much eating and drinking. We celebrated as we once did at home in Alexanderhausen, before the communist economy was imposed on us.

We continued our drive to Ulm, where we visited cousin Hermann and family in Neu Ulm. A few compatriots came to visit and again we had an emotional reunion with them, because we had not seen each other for more than 25 years. Cousin Hilde came from Stuttgart, where she lived with her family. Next we drove to the Austrian village of Unterrach am Attersee, where we visited another distant cousin. From there it was just a day trip through Budapest to Neusiedl am See, where the landscape was already beginning to remind me of the Banat. From there we wanted to leave early, so that we would reach Temeswar the following day, before nightfall. We had been warned of possible delays at the border crossing Nagylak/Nădlac, and we thought that we had made sufficient allowance for the expected long queues.

When we arrived at the border early in the afternoon, the line of cars appeared to be manageable. We could see the border station in Romania and watch the proceedings there. A truck driver from England, who had used this border crossing many times before, assured us that by nine o'clock we would have the customs clearance behind us. But it was slow progress, so that we reached the village of Nădlac only around two o'clock in the morning. The street lighting in the village consisted of a single fluorescent tube in front of the town hall. Driving in the dark, we found the only hotel in town, but it was closed. No one answered our knocks and shaking of the door. Donna was adamantly opposed to a drive on the dark country road towards Arad, so we spent the night in our rental car, parked in the parking lot of the hotel. We tried to sleep, but none of us really succeeded. It was the first night in their lives that our boys spent in a car instead of a bed.

At the first sign of dawn, we continued our drive through Arad and reached the Continental Hotel in Temeswar just before noon. When we stumbled more than walked through the entrance hall, Konrad had to vomit. No one cared and we went on to the elevators. These were not working and we had to lug our bags up the stairs. According to a notice stuck to the bathroom wall, there should have been warm water at this time. But there was no warm water and when we crawled into our beds, we felt tired and neither clean nor refreshed.

We slept through the afternoon and the night. Breakfast was a new experience, especially for the boys. There was no orange juice or fruit juice; all we could get was mineral water from Busiaş. It came in beer bottles and in one of them swam small scraps of paper. This bottle was exchanged at our request. Then we could order cold eggs, bacon and a kind of sausage. The boys only ate bread slices with the same jam of mixed fruits that I still remembered from my student days.

After breakfast we went to the nearby Cathedral Square and visited our old and venerable cathedral. The day was very hot and after lunch our boys wanted only to sleep and not leave the hotel room. I took a walk to the city centre by myself, and reached the Corso through an underpass. It was very different from its image in my memory. I visited a nearby grocery store and found long shelves filled with bottles of mineral water. The vendor admitted that all of the displayed brands contained sulphur and would not really be suitable for drinking. I bought a packet of biscuits and returned to the hotel. I wanted to call some colleagues, but a telephone book was nowhere to be found.

The next day we all got in our rental car and drove to Alexanderhausen. There were very few vehicles on the Szegedin highway and I was amazed how quickly we reached the village. We found my aunt and cousin working in their well-cultivated garden. They were not surprised by our arrival, since they had learned about our trip from our common relatives in Rastatt. We were invited for lunch, and after a short rest we all went across the street to the cemetery. The grave of my aunt's family was well maintained and full of flowers, the way I remembered the graves in our village cemetery. Oma's nearby grave was reduced to a small handful of dust, gathered near its marble cross. I had not expected flowers on the grave, but a few minutes of hoeing once a year would at least have kept its outline recognizable.

My aunt had noticed my shock, because on the way back from the cemetery, and even when we said our goodbyes, I could hardly utter a word. She seemed to smile to herself, because after almost thirty years, she had finally settled her accounts with us. She had obviously retained her feeling that during my years as a student in Temeswar I had neglected to visit her and her family often enough. She blamed either Oma or me, or both of us, for that perceived lack of respect. But did she remember the time when Oma wanted to borrow 500 Lei from her, and my aunt turned her down? Now she had at last found the opportunity to get back at all of us, the living and the dead: She had not lifted a finger to maintain our grave, at least in its outline.

On our return trip, we crossed the border once again at Nădlac. There we were shocked to witness the treatment of an old man by a Romanian border guard. The man appeared to be on his way to Hungary by bicycle, and a search of his person seemed to have found some prohibited item or items. The border guard treated him with a selection of the crudest Romanian curses, uttered in such a loud voice, that everyone in the neighbourhood must have heard them. Then he sent the old man back to Romania, screaming loudly after him: "We know how to deal with you and your kind!"

Back in Ottawa, the handful of dust in the cemetery of Alexanderhausen would just not get out of my mind. I wrote a letter to my cousin and her husband, asking them to have a concrete cover placed over our grave, as had been done with most graves belonging to Swabians who had left. I naturally offered to bear the costs of this operation and settle them in any way they wished. But I was not surprised when I received no reply to that letter.

At the time, my friend Richard was still employed as a chemical engineer in a state-owned enterprise located near Cluj, in Transylvania. When I wrote him about my experience with my aunt and my cousin, he immediately offered to look into the matter. On a visit to Alexanderhausen, he arranged to have a concrete cover placed over Oma's grave, so that it did no longer require maintenance and looked like most of the graves surrounding it. I was deeply touched by this act of friendship and generosity, for which Richard absolutely refused to send me the bill.

# 40. Professional conferences

In 1982 I had the opportunity to write and present a technical paper at the professional conference of my peers, taking place in Washington. It was a conference of experts and researchers in the field of energy provision to telecommunication systems. Two years later I wrote and presented a second technical paper. In 1986, when the conference took place in Toronto, I was invited to become a member of the Program Committee, a small group responsible for setting up the technical program of the conference. At the same time, I prepared a presentation and participated actively in the discussions that followed the presentation of each technical paper.

The conference became an international success, attracting every year about 600 to 1000 participants from all over the world. Now it took place every year, always one year in North America and the following year anywhere in the world. When I look at the volumes of conference proceedings, I am reminded that over the years I attended conferences in Washington, New Orleans, Toronto, Stockholm, San Diego, Florence, Orlando, Kyoto, again Washington, Paris, Vancouver, The Hague, Boston, Melbourne, San Francisco, Phoenix, Montreal, Chicago, and Providence. At the last three conferences I participated as a pensioner.

At most meetings I acted as chairman of at least one technical session, and at many of them I also presented a technical paper. Later on I continued to represent my company on one or more committees. In preparation for the meetings held in North America, the members of the Technical Program Committee usually met several months before the date of the conference, to review and approve the submitted abstracts of the proposed papers and to put together a sound technical program. These meetings were held in a city in the U.S.A. or Canada, chosen by the members of the committee.

The ITU (International Telecommunication Union) is an agency of the United Nations that regulates the areas of information and communication technology. After the meeting in Florence, it hosted a meeting of the sub-division of ITU for developing battery standards. In Ottawa, I had received the authority to represent Canada on this forum. It was a meeting of the battery experts from many countries in the West and in the East. I was proud to wear the designation "Canada" on my name tag. I felt something like compassion for the representatives of the Soviet Union and Eastern Bloc countries, because they did not understand English and depended on the time-consuming simultaneous translation. I had visited the famous cathedral of Florence (the Duomo) on the day before the start of the conference. I also found time for a brief visit to the renowned picture gallery (Galeria degli Uffizi). I resolved firmly to myself that I would return there one day, when I had more time to admire all the masterpieces.

In Tokyo, the underground city train run like clockwork, so that I could use it to take in some of the sights of the great city. Two days later I took the Shinkansen high speed train to Kyoto, the venue for our conference. Before the start of the meeting, I found just a little time to visit some of the most famous temples. Our hosts, the Japanese Organizing Committee, invited our committee members to dinner in a traditional Japanese restaurant. We sat around the room on little chairs near ground level, with each of us facing a little table. No fewer than 14 courses were served, with tea, Kirin beer, warm sake and cold sake. At our hotel, hot water for tea was brought to the hotel room every afternoon around four o'clock.

Donna accompanied me to the conference in Australia. In Sydney we had three free days to visit the city and its surroundings as tourists. We continued on to Melbourne, where the conference took place in a modern conference centre. At the banquet, an orchestra played and we danced to the strains of "Waltzing Matilda", Australia's most famous bush ballad, folk song, and the "unofficial national anthem of Australia". I had been able to squeeze in a vacation week following the conference. We flew to Cairns, a popular tourist destination with a tropical climate, surrounded by many attractions. We spent the week with trips to the rainforest and the Great Barrier Reef. We reached the coral reef by catamaran, in about an hour. Placing the mask of a snorkelling set on the surface of the water was like looking into a giant aquarium. There was a profusion of brightly colored coral, surrounded by a variety of fish of different shapes and colors.

Donna went on to accompany me to all subsequent conferences, until we decided that the meeting in Providence (state of Rhode Island) taking place during 2006 would be our last one. During the previous six years of retirement, my interest had gradually turned to a hitherto neglected area, namely the life of my ancestors and the history of the Danube Swabians in general.

# 41. THE NINETEEN NINETIES

Another unexpected opportunity came along in the nineties. As a technical adviser, I was asked to look after the interests of my company in the development of industry standards for the energy supply to telecommunication equipment. At the beginning it was only an additional assignment, but later on it took a lot of my time and brought with it frequent travel to meetings in many cities in the USA and Canada.

These industry standards set limits for the voltages at which alternating current was supplied from the commercial power grid or generated by diesel alternators, for charging and discharging of batteries, as well as limits for the voltage within which the communications equipment would have to operate normally. Limits were also specified for the electromagnetic interference produced by the telecommunications equipment, and for the external electromagnetic interference that our equipment would have to tolerate. Finally, there were requirements for lead-acid batteries and other batteries, and for the operational and safety grounding of various facilities.

The standards were issued by agencies such as ANSI (American Standards Institute) and CSA (Canadian Standards Association). Additional requirements were added later to coordinate the North American standards with those of the ETSI (European Telecommunications Standards Institute) and ITU-Telecom. As already mentioned, the ITU (International Telecommunications Union) is an agency of the United Nations, which regulates issues of information and communication technology. The tasks assigned to us by this agency were usually resolved by written submissions, with occasional joint meetings coordinated with the professional conferences attended by many of the subject matter experts involved.

The tasks assigned to us by agencies such as ANSI and CSA made joint meetings necessary. The experts from all parts of the United States and Canada scheduled monthly meetings to work out the major issues and reach consensus on the provisions of the standards. To keep the travel costs reasonable for all participants, the meetings were held in different cities across the continent. The duration of each of these meetings was three or four days, with the participants usually travelling on weekends.

Often there was not enough free time available to get more than a superficial impression of a city. Sometimes one could use a Saturday or Sunday to get to know the city better. In Canada, I participated in meetings in Vancouver, Calgary, Toronto, Montreal, Halifax and St. John's. The list of cities located in the United States is longer, but I can certainly remember the following: Miami, Orlando, St. Augustine, New Orleans, Charlotte, Richmond, Baltimore, Washington, New York, Boston, Milwaukee, Minneapolis, Kansas City, Houston, San Antonio, Denver, Salt Lake City, Phoenix, San Diego, Los Angeles, San Francisco, and Seattle.

The meetings in New York were actually held in a hotel in the suburbs, because the city itself and all events taking place in it were considered to be very expensive. We also avoided Las Vegas, mainly because it was understood that people go there for the gambling and not for doing useful work. The choice of the meeting place was also dependent on the availability of a voluntary host, a role usually assumed by one of the larger operating companies in the field of telecommunications.

I also have fond memories of a meeting that took place in a ski resort near Denver. The city itself is already located 5280 feet (1600 meters) above sea level, and from there it was still a nearly two hour long drive up into the mountains. No wonder that the car rental agency at the airport, after I had indicated my destination, assigned me a car with four-wheel drive and a powerful engine. Before arriving at the resort, there were several sharp hairpin bends in the road. During the next few days we could all feel the thin air and some participants experienced real problems with it.

Park City, Utah, is a beautifully situated ski resort, accessible by car from the Salt Lake City airport. On a rare free afternoon, three of us drove back from Park City to Salt Lake City, over a fairly narrow mountain road. We wanted to see the city and the temple of the Mormons. We knew that the Mormons were proud to have saved more than 4 billion genealogical records, the world's largest collection of family research data. We visited the centre for family research and I quickly found some valuable data about some of my ancestors. My efforts in family research actually began with these data.

# 42. OTHER UNIVERSITIES

During these busy and hectic years, our two boys successfully completed their secondary schooling. Now it became important to find the most suitable universities for them. It was certainly an exciting time for the boys and perhaps even more for us parents.

Raimund graduated from one of the oldest and most prestigious high schools in Ottawa and sent his application for admission to three universities located in the province of Ontario. On the advice of his professors, he also sent his application to two elite universities in the United States. Soon he received an acceptance letter with generous scholarship offers from universities in Toronto, Hamilton and Ottawa.

But before he could opt for one of these universities, he received an offer of admission from Harvard University in Cambridge, near Boston. Although this offer brought him immediate congratulations from his professors and colleagues, it also created some concern for us parents. From the 12,000 applications received for that year, Harvard had to select 1,200 candidates. To find the most suitable candidates without discrimination, the university used so-called "need-free admission". This approach takes into account only the proven performance of each candidate, without regard to the financial situation or solvency of the applicant and his family.

We knew that a year of study at Harvard University, including tuition, room and board, books and extracurricular activities, cost around 25,000 U.S. dollars. Now the university demanded data such as my annual income, my tax return, my savings and my bank accounts. Based on these data, its financial experts determined how much our family could pay without experiencing financial hardships. To make up the required sum, the university offered a scholarship, a loan repayable after graduation, and a paid part-time job within the university. This allocation reduced the share to be paid by the parents to a tolerable level. We accepted the offer and Raimund enrolled at Harvard University.

At the opening of the first academic year, some professors were making presentations geared especially to parents. All of these professors demonstrated a sovereign mastery of their subject matter and were also brilliant speakers. In his address, the President of Harvard introduced the example of a student called Miller. For his thesis, Miller had to establish whether a known historical event was to be rated as positive or negative. In the conclusions of his work, the student wrote something like, ". . . Historians need to make further inquiries into this event . . ." When he defended his thesis and reached those lines, the professor took off his glasses and said: "But Mr. Miller, we are the historians". The speech left no doubt in the minds of the listeners, that the professors of this university were in fact the historians, writers, scientists and scholars who often had the last word in their areas of competence.

Raimund was now looking forward to four years of study, and he chose history as the subject of his concentration. He achieved excellent results that led to additional grants, such as the John Harvard Scholarship and the Harvard College Scholarship. In his spare time, Raimund was working a few hours a week at the Central Library of the University, which was busy creating an online catalogue of the 12 million books available in its 52 branches. He found the work very interesting and earned some pocket money, but the family contribution to the tuition fees changed very little. Raimund joined the Canadian Club, together with his Canadian peers, including the son of one of the richest families in Canada and the daughter of a prime minister. I could not help but admire the institutions of the United States and Canada, whose gates were wide open to the son of an immigrant, based only on his proven capabilities, achievements and readiness to work.

For the summer after his first year, Raimund received a grant from the Sörös Foundation to spend his vacation teaching English in Transylvania. He spent the subsequent two summers in Europe working for the travel guide "Let's Go" which was published in several languages by a group of Harvard students. In the first of these years, he wrote about Czechoslovakia; the following year he researched Croatia, western Hungary and Slovenia. From his short-lease rented apartment in Budapest and Prague, respectively, he traveled through the regions and countries of his interest. For the summer before his graduation, Raimund received another grant, this time for a study trip to Europe, to research material relevant to his thesis in the libraries of Vienna, Budapest, Temeswar/Timisoara and Fünfkirchen/ Pécs.

Raimund's thesis was entitled "Constructing a Civic National Identity - Magyar and Swabian Nation-Builders in Hungary 1760-1848". His conclusion was something like this: "By confining political activity to the cultural sphere and thus rendering voluntary cultural Magyarization as the principal way of expressing Hungarian political interests, the harsh Habsburg neo-absolutism of the 1850s seriously hindered the development of a civic Hungarian national identity." It is easy to agree with that conclusion, but the word "voluntary" could certainly stand further clarification.

Two of his three evaluators, including Professor Roman Szporluk, rated this work with "magna cum laude plus". Raimund graduated the same year and was awarded the Bachelor of Arts academic degree, with the attribute "magna cum laude". A graduation with such high honours deserved to be celebrated by the whole family. Donna, Konrad and I travelled to Cambridge by car and took part in a unique graduation ceremony, displaying the multiple resources and talents available to the renowned Harvard University that had been graduating students since 1636.

Raimund now faced the question whether to join the workforce or continue his studies. He knew that Harvard would welcome him as a graduate student of history. The realization that the content of this study would be not so much a comprehensive knowledge of world history, but a thorough grounding in modern historiography, certainly influenced his decision against undertaking four years of graduate study. Raimund decided to study law instead and enrolled at the Law Centre of the Georgetown University in Washington. This university, founded by the Jesuits, is known as a training ground for diplomats in Washington. After three years he received his Juris Doctor (Doctor of Law) and was hired by a large law firm in San Francisco. When many of the local high-tech companies became victims of the collapse of 2000, his law firm lost many of its customers. Raimund moved to southern California, where he continued his work as a lawyer in the greater Los Angeles area.

One can safely assume that his interest in history, world history and the history of the Danube Swabians remains alive. Whether and if he will find the time and inclination for further studies in these areas, only time will tell. There is always the possibility that such efforts will have to await his retirement.

Konrad, our younger son, had spent the last four years before graduating from high school at a newly built high school in our neighbourhood. He also followed the procedures established by the province and sent his application for admission simultaneously to three Ontario universities of his choice. He received letters of acceptance with offers of scholarships from the University of Waterloo and Carleton University of Ottawa. We travelled to Waterloo and visited its Faculty of Mathematics and Computer Science. This faculty is well respected across the continent and its graduates are often offered positions by the major American computer firms, such as Microsoft and International Business Machines (IBM).

Konrad chose Carleton University, whose faculty of computer science also had a good reputation. He continued to live at home with his parents and had to put up with a daily hour-long bus ride to the university. His scholarship was renewed for each of the four years of study. He participated in so-called "cooperative studies" under which the University arranged summer employment for him, at some of the local computer companies. In addition to being directly relevant to his studies, these placements were also well remunerated, so that Konrad needed very little financial support from his parents to complete his university studies.

He graduated in 1999 with a Bachelor of Science degree in Computer Science and Mathematics. He immediately started in a well-paid job as a software developer at the local high-tech company, where he had spent a semester as a cooperative student. Two years later, when technology companies collapsed left and right, he lost his job, along with many of his colleagues. His short high flight ended with a tragic and undeserved crash into the abyss. Our feelings as parents can best be summed up with the statement that the jealous gods had once again denied a mortal the access to their Mount Olympus.

# 43. A NEW CENTURY

I had not heard from my old friend Robert for a long time, when he suddenly called in the spring of 2000. He was in Ottawa, where he had found a trusted doctor, whom he was planning to visit monthly. He still lived in the Montreal area, with his wife and two sons. I invited him to dinner, for which Donna was happy to prepare a meal reminiscent of the Banat. Robert praised the food, but drank no beer or wine. He said that he liked good food, even if it was not conducive to his diabetes.

After dinner Robert and I were sitting in our living room, talking about the turns our lives had taken in Canada. It was rather sad that this was his first visit with my family and that I had never met his family. He had worked many years in the oil fields of Alberta and in several foreign countries. He had spent many of his holidays in Europe, as his in-laws made their home in Switzerland. Our connection had been reduced to the occasional letter and phone calls. We regretted this state of affairs, but we knew that we were not the only ones of our compatriots experiencing a weakening of the social and personal ties among themselves.

We recounted the events of the past. The Old Canadians of Montreal had spent their first years in apartment buildings located in the city center, near the St. Bonifatius Church. Living close together, they saw each other almost daily. The women talked to each other almost daily, as they had done back home in the Banat. After working hours, the men often met in a neighbourhood tavern or for a card game in one of their apartments. On Sunday they went to church, just as they had done back home in the Banat. Once the age of the car started, they could drive from their homes to their workplaces anywhere in the city and its surroundings. As the city expanded, the new settlements were built farther and farther from the city centre. Not even the fact that the city was located on an island could limit this expansion, as new suburbs were built on its south shore as well as on its north shore.

Our countrymen arriving in Montreal after the Second World War found their first living quarters in many parts of the city. Later on, virtually all of them had cars and bought new houses in ever more remote districts, where they could be bought at affordable prices. The result was that our countrymen lived apart from each other and rarely came together. Some people still went to church on Sundays, while others went only rarely or not at all. The older people met occasionally at funerals and at Christmas or New Year's celebrations in the church halls. The members of the younger generation had found their own friends and forms of entertainment.

Robert and I regretted this state of affairs, but could not see any alternative to it. Robert's father had died eleven years ago and his mother had followed him four years later. After selling his farm in the Eastern Townships and moving back to Montreal, Anton Schwarz had died in 1967. His wife, Theresia, continued to live for another twenty years. With their son Peter, who had moved to Toronto, Robert and I exchanged only Christmas cards, sometimes with short messages written on their back.

After promising each other to keep up our relationship and see each other more often, I drove Robert to the station, from which he took the bus home. I could not stop thinking about the many people who had either left this earth, or with whom we had simply lost the connection. Almost all of its German inhabitants had left our home village of Alexanderhausen. Relatives and neighbours had emigrated over the decades, most of them to Germany. There, the younger ones lived scattered across the country. Many of the older men and women had died. In his Christmas letter of 1968, Richard reported the death of his grandfather Lorenz. Richard himself had to await the end of the dictatorship in Romania, before he could emigrate to Germany.

While living in Ottawa, it often took years before I found out that one or another of our compatriots in Montreal or Southern Ontario had died. Uncle Nick lived to a ripe old age and died only in 2001, two years after the death of his wife, my aunt.

I learned of the death of Mrs. Beck in 1975; her husband had already died in 1967. The timber merchant Glass had lived in Germany until his death in 1973. Uncle Gerhard also spent his last years in Germany, where he died in 1971. The life of my Schneider Uncle ended in Baden Baden in 1976, and his wife followed him in 1984, after a short illness. The two men from Alexanderhausen, who had gone to England as prisoners of war and stayed there, had disappeared from the radar screens of their compatriots. Nobody seemed to know anything about their lives and deaths.

Robert and I had now reached the age in which many contemporaries read the obituaries in the newspaper, not only to find out who had died, but to be reassured that their names were not listed. In November 2009 I received the sad news that Robert had died at the age of 73.

# 44. One more visit to the Banat

In June 2008 Donna and I returned to Temeswar for the fiftieth anniversary of my graduation from the Technical University Politehnica Timisoara, still called Polytechnikum by the few Banat Swabians still living in the city and in the surrounding villages. The spring sun was shining down from a cloudless sky when our airplane landed at the "Traian Vuia" airport of Timisoara and came to a full stop between planes marked "Carpatair" and "Air Moldova". The drive into the city took longer than expected, because the road was full of cars, from old Dacias to brand new BMWs. The city spread out before us in the bright sunshine seemed familiar yet somehow strange. The large pedestrian zone in the centre, from the State Opera to the Orthodox Cathedral, was full of people and pigeons. People did not walk up and down the Corso as they once did, but mostly sat on the benches in the gardens, with a beer or coffee in front of them. I was pleasantly surprised that the restaurant Lloyd, once the finest in the city, had resumed its operation.

The Cathedral Square (Domplatz) was mostly closed to traffic, but the street next to the Serbian Orthodox Cathedral was full of parked cars. There were cars parked on both sides of the smaller streets, some with two wheels on the sidewalk. The Mass just being celebrated in our Catholic Cathedral was entirely in the Romanian language. Some of the historic buildings which surround Cathedral Square had been restored and looked splendid, while others were still awaiting their restoration.

In downtown Temeswar we found money changers or banks on almost every street corner. Unfortunately, the banks were closed on that Saturday and none of the small exchange bureaus were willing to exchange my travelers' checks for Romanian currency. We had to wait until Monday morning when we finally found a bank willing to process the exchange. To do so, the clerk inspected my passport and wrote down my Canadian address, completed three forms in duplicate and asked me to sign each one of them. After deducting two percent for his efforts, he finally handed me the Romanian currency.

The Rectorate of the Technical University was still located in its magnificent building dating back to the time of the Austro-Hungarian double monarchy. The official part of our meeting was held in the very impressive new Great Hall of the Rectorate building. In the afternoon, all participants took a touring bus to the village of Rekasch. Awaiting us at the local winery was a very good meal, accompanied by several varieties of "Swabian wine". We toured the facilities and the wine cellars, where our tour guide praised the Banat Swabians as the founders of viticulture in Rekasch.

The next day we walked through the Josefstadt, in the footsteps of my school and university years spent in that part of the city. It was still obvious that my former student residence located across from the Catholic Church of the Josefstadt had once been a beautiful upper-class apartment building. Unfortunately, looking at it stirred up memories of the bedbugs that I had encountered there. I sincerely hoped that whoever lived there now did not have to put up with such pests.

The weekly market of the Josefstadt now takes place in covered halls. The breakfast in our hotel had already convinced us that the peppers, tomatoes and cucumbers grown in the Banat were still among the tastiest in the world. Unfortunately there were no more Banat-Swabian women selling these vegetables in the market. The new Timisoara North railway station building was completely new and unfamiliar to me, because I knew only its predecessor. On the street in front of the station, we could make out a rather small two-star hotel. It had served as our dormitory during the student uprising in October 1956. Even today I could not erase from memory the image of the machine gun standing in the middle of its entrance hall.

We visited the "Museum of the Banat" housed in the venerable Hunyadi Castle. Among other documents, we admired a copy of the Declaration of Alba Iulia, regarding the incorporation of Transylvania and the Banat into Greater Romania. We did not find any update on how the minority rights promised by that declaration were applied in practice during the years that followed. On another day we went to the city forest, once known as "Jagdwald" or "hunting woods". On our way there we saw many pompous homes belonging to absent Romas or gypsies. The locals called these buildings "gypsy palaces". In the "hunting woods" we also visited, among others, a "German farmhouse" at the Museum of the Village. It had brand new gutters, but unfortunately no pillared corridor facing the yard.

Following the generous invitation of a colleague, we were able to attend a performance of "Gypsy Baron" at the State Opera. It stirred up powerful memories of the many opera performances that I had attended in this beautiful hall. How many performances of "Die Fledermaus" by Johann Strauss had I attended on New Year's Eve? Colleagues who had never left Timisoara told me that the history of the city and the Banat was now being seen differently. It is now recognized that the Dual Monarchy was not a "prison of nations" as had been claimed in earlier times, but rather a significant contributor to the development of the city and the region. Even the erstwhile peaceful coexistence of the various nationalities in the Banat is now seen as an early example of the Europe of the future.

My colleague was kind enough to take us on a drive to Alexanderhausen. On our way out of Temeswar I recognized the place where the Arad and Torontal highways come together. In the first half of the 1950s this junction was the location of the large depot of Soviet tanks. In October 1956, the tanks made their way from here to Budapest, traveling along the same Szegedin highway on which we were now traveling at almost 100 kilometres per hour.

The trees were still standing on both of its sides, but the road was now covered with asphalt. We left the former Neubeschenowa on our right, and drove through Kleinbetschkerek. In the fields to our right we were surprised to see a large flock of sheep with a Romanian shepherd, just as I remembered them from decades ago.

After a few minutes we reached the village of Billed. Soon after, the familiar two steeples arose from the green of the heath. From a distance they appeared as friendly as in the days when Alexanderhausen was still a Swabian village. The village seemed completely covered in green, with trees, shrubs, and grass covering every unpaved speck of land. There was hardly a trace of the former trenches that once had a role in coping with floods or high water levels. They had either been deliberately levelled, or the grass had overwhelmed them. The ponds had either disappeared or had gradually flattened out. Apparently there is no longer any risk of high ground water levels. Of the two rows of mulberry trees on each side of the street, only a few remnants could be seen. Most of the trees were probably removed when party and government had ordered the people to plant vegetable gardens in front of their houses. The area taken by the 20 fathoms (about 38 meters) wide streets were supposed to provide food for the socialist society.

Our first steps led us to the cemetery on the Neusiedel/Uihei side of the village, to the graveside of my family. It is the grave that I had often visited with Oma, where she had finally found her eternal rest. It was now covered by a slab of concrete, as I knew it would be, similar to most of the tombs of the departed Banat Swabians. The ruin of the chapel stood there in the shade, and looked as if it could last for several more years.

On the meadows located on the southern corner of the village, there were chickens and crows, just like in those summer days of long ago, when this was our favourite summer playground. The railway crossing was no longer there, and neither was the railway bridge, which once played an important role in the system of ditches. The dug-out lower sections also appeared levelled here, and they were covered with grass, as they were everywhere else in the village. We drove to the place where our house once stood, the place where I was born and where my family once lived. In its place we found a half-finished building, built from a kind of brick. The Romanian neighbour told us that it belonged to a Romanian living in America. The garden was planted with corn, as far as one could see. Some of the houses once owned by Banat Swabians were inhabited and kept in good condition; others seemed to be uninhabited and abandoned. Of some, only ruins could be seen, and others had disappeared without traces.

We drove to the church and parked the car nearby. The church door was locked and clearly needed repair. The school had been enlarged and appeared well maintained. The former Great Inn looked like it was in urgent need of repair. We went to the "Pension Schwabenhaus" which was actually built around the house of a former Swabian farmer. The rooms were impeccably furnished, the restaurant looked comfortable and friendly, and the "multi-functional" hall for 150 people looked impressive. Museum objects such as Swabian clocks, mortars and farm implements could be admired throughout the property. Domestic and imported beers and wines were readily available, at prices comparable to those in the West.

I had always wanted to visit Lenauheim, with its old monument dedicated to the poet Nikolaus Lenau and its heritage museum of newer vintage. At the Schwabenhaus we were told that the shorter route via Neusiedel and Bogarosch was barely passable for cars. We were advised to continue on the Szegedin highway to Lowrin, and then take the road to Gottlob and Grabatz, and from there to Lenauheim. Outside one of the villages we came across a familiar picture: a large pond with little water and a lot of geese.

We drove along the main street of Lenauheim, and soon after passing the Catholic church the museum appeared on the right side of the road. The birthplace of the poet, once built for the imperial and royal administration of Austria-Hungary, was an impressive and well-maintained building. The woman in charge of the building spoke Romanian and German, and was as familiar with the biography of the poet as with the history of the Banat Swabians. The rooms of the museum were arranged to emulate typical rooms of a Banat-Swabian farmer's house: kitchen, bedroom, and storage room, all furnished with furniture, carpets, blankets, pillows, wall hangings, dishes, cutlery, pictures, spinning wheels and other items usually found in farm house and its annexes. Even clothing typical of the older generations was hanging on a "board with taps".

In the rooms dedicated to Nikolaus Lenau one could see early editions of his books, translations of his poems in several languages, photos and documents. Hanging on the walls were quotes from the poet in German and Romanian. The initial enthusiasm of the poet for America and his later disappointment aroused mixed feelings in a traveler from Canada: Heaven could not be found anywhere on earth then and it cannot be found now. Although his life had led Lenau out of the Banat at an early age, many of his poems reflect the melancholy that will always resonate in the consciousness of the Banat Swabians, wherever they may be living today.

Leaving Lenauheim, we reached the Hatzfed—Temeswar highway at Gertianosch. We drove through Sackelhausen, which already looked like a suburb of Temeswar, and were back in Temeswar before the evening fell. We concluded that the Banat had become very small indeed in the age of the car.

Two days later we boarded an aircraft that took us back to München, and then another one that brought us back home to Canada. My thoughts, however, remained in the Banat for a good while longer. Our grandfathers once had to take their potatoes to the market in Temeswar by horse-drawn wagons. Sometimes they had to spend the night at the inn at Tschoka-Puszta. Our fathers needed to take their potatoes for export only to the railway station of Alexanderhausen. My generation finally were the commuters, who took the morning train into the city and returned to the village with the evening train. Today the car is king, and it drastically reduced the apparent size of the Banat. By car, one can easily traverse the former undivided Banat in one day. But the greatest miracle that makes such a trip possible is that the borders are finally open, after they had been closed for so many years.

The idea, that this could have been my last encounter with my former homeland Banat, lingered in my mind for a long time. I tried to keep the hope alive in my heart, that at least in our cemeteries, the graves of our ancestors will endure for all time.

# 45. In conclusion

There is very little sand left in the upper half of the hourglass of our life. Our time in this world is running out. Our role on the world stage is nearly played out and we are slowly leaving the stage. We were called the experience generation, because we experienced the disastrous war and had to bear its consequences. Too many of us had to endure the loss of our parents, siblings or other loved ones. In the end we even lost our ancestral homeland, the Banat. On the surface, these wounds appear healed, but deep down the pain persists until the day we die.

The most sublime experiences of my life were without doubt the birth and growing up of our boys. When our children meet and even surpass the silent, never expressed hopes and expectations of their parents, we feel fulfilled. We feel the satisfaction of having done something right in life, and that enhances the meaning of life. Our children are our novels, our symphonies; they give their parents that immortality, which is placed in the cradle of every person. When the children grow up and become adults, they have the opportunity of writing their own novels and their own symphonies in the book of life. In this way, what is received is passed on from one generation to the next, and an inherent meaning of life is realized. WE become part of an endless stream extending from the dim past into a hopefully brighter future.

From the depths of the subconscious sometimes arises the question: Did my life run along the best possible course? Had the conditions in the world been different, life could have taken many of us in different directions. But we could not influence the external circumstances ourselves; they were determined by the coordinates of our existence in space and time. The childhood in a peaceful and safe village will always remain a happy memory. The disastrous war cast its shadow on my youth. It raged like a severe storm in the plains, with its dark clouds often covering the sun. But there were always books to be read, and their beauty and wisdom often brought consolation in the hours of despair. The universe continued to follow its eternal rules and logic, which had been uncovered by some mathematical geniuses. The world still followed its eternal laws and logical progressions, and it was a privilege to learn about and understand some of these laws. That made it easier to avoid despair about the world around us, in which irrationality and brutality prevailed, and which we were powerless to change.

Sometimes, very seldom, the question may arise as to why one could not have experienced more good days, why one had to live through days of sorrow and worry. Would it have been possible to make one's life easier? Were some hard days perhaps self-inflicted? In retrospect, these questions must be answered in the negative. Virtually all of our difficult and depressing days were imposed on us by the circumstances, some would say by fate. It would be futile and in vain to ponder them today. We should be making better use of the remaining days of our lives. As a prerequisite for that, we must accept that everything happened the way it had to happen.

It would be a wonderful feeling to be able to say that the world is a better place on our departure than it was during our short time on this earth. It is very sad indeed that we cannot say that. New dangers have come into the world, more dangerous weapons and, unfortunately, more dangerous people. We can only wish mankind the best of luck for its long-term survival. We must keep up our hope that mankind will prevail, as it has time and again throughout its history.

You can not go home again; there is no road that leads you back to the home that you once knew. This has been rightfully said of people who had left their homes voluntarily, under normal circumstances, and whose physical return was, at least in principle, possible at any time. How much more does it apply to us, those who had to leave our home under the pressure of circumstances that were beyond our control.

About our new country that welcomed us and gave us a chance for a new beginning and a new life, we can only say: Many came, saw and returned to a homeland that was still saddened by their departure. Others stayed on, however, and this vast country slowly became their own country, and this continent became their home.

When the end comes, there will be no brass band to play the March of the Dead, that haunting melody of unspeakable sadness that once echoed across the village from the cemetery of Alexanderhausen. West of the city of Ottawa, almost in the small community of Carp, our last home awaits my family in a small cemetery. Only a modest grave stone of granite will bear our names, including the name of a man born a few decades earlier in the lowlands of the Banat. There is hope that on these forty square feet of Canadian soil he will finally find eternal peace, surrounded by those who loved him and whom he loved.

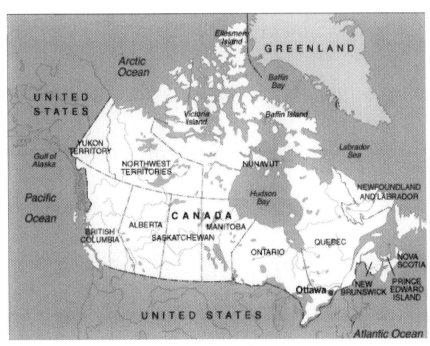

Map of Canada